The Best
Competitions for
talented
kids

The Best
Competitions for
talented
kids

**Win Scholarships,
Big Prize Money,
and Recognition**

*Best Wishes!
Frances A. Karnes*

Frances A. Karnes, Ph.D., & Tracy L. Riley, Ph.D.

PRUFROCK PRESS INC.
WACO, TEXAS

For our grandchildren,
Mary Ryan, Mo, Emma, Brooks, and Betsy Karnes and Preston
Gowland-Riley, and for all other children and youth who celebrate
their talents through competition. May each of you use every
opportunity available to become the best possible you!

Prufrock Press Inc.
P.O. Box 8813
Waco, TX 76714-8813
Phone: (800) 998-2208
Fax: (800) 240-0333
http://www.prufrock.com

table of contents

table of contents

introduction

competitions:
what you should know

Have you ever created a great invention, worked on a science experiment, written an intriguing mystery, developed a webpage, or led a service project for your community? Through competitions, you can use your skills and win in many ways. Entering competitions can be a fun and exciting part of your life.

Competition has become the backbone of our society. Adults engage in informal and formal competition nearly every day. Yet, only in the last two to three decades have competitions at the national level been available to youth. When young people participate in competitions, they are preparing to be productive adults.

There are a variety of national and international competitions identified in this book. There likely will be several in which you'll want to participate. You will discover great things about competitions. By participating, you will learn more about yourself and your special talents and abilities. Academic talents, such as those in language arts, science, mathematics, and social studies, as well as talents in the fine and performing arts (e.g., drawing, painting, theater, and photography), can be further developed. Leadership and service learning in your school and community offer special opportunities to get involved. Most competitions in this book are open to any student, but a few require membership in an organization. Whatever your interests, this book offers a variety of competitions in which to participate.

who will benefit from this book

This book is written for elementary and secondary students. However, there are others who will also benefit from using it. Teachers will want to know the wide variety of competitions available and how to prepare their students to compete. Parents will find the number and variety of competitions of interest and will find the specifics provided helpful in assisting their children in making appropriate choices for competing. Guidance counselors and school librarians will be able to use the information to help students find appropriate outlets for their talents, as will youth group directors wanting to involve students in a wide variety of positive endeavors. Share this book with teachers, parents, or other adults who can help you and your friends become involved in competitions.

how competitions were selected for this book

Competitions for elementary and secondary students focusing on academics, creativity, fine and performing arts, leadership, and service learning were selected for inclusion in this book. Although there are many ways to compete within your community and state, we thought having information on national competitions would help you to know about alternate ways in which to participate. It was important that most of the competitions listed have no entrance fee, although some do require one. Much time and effort were given to locating the listed competitions. Competition sponsors also had the opportunity to submit information about their event. A few competitions chose not to be included or were uncertain of their funding for the future. If you know of competitions not listed here, please let us know for the next edition.

how to use this book

This book is divided into three sections. Part I includes 150 competitions ranging from mythology to visual arts. The competitions are listed in alphabetical order. Part II is a Competitions Journal, which provides reproducible pages for you to record your ideas about competitions. You will have an opportunity to set goals for competition, reflect upon your feelings, and investigate new areas of interest. Part III is a list of resources that will help you as you prepare for competitions. There are books that offer everything, from how to give a speech to how to sharpen your skills as a photographer.

thanks! thanks! thanks!

We would like to give special thanks to the individuals and groups who have been helpful in taking an idea and turning it into a book. We owe an enormous debt of gratitude to those adults who have conducted competitions and contributed information.

We would like to acknowledge The University of Southern Mississippi and Massey University for the support they have given us during the writing of this book.

We thank Rachel Taliaferro, our editor, for her ideas and insights. To Joel McIntosh, our publisher, we are very grateful for his interest in our ideas and for his positive personality and futuristic thinking.

Our families are constantly helpful and supportive of our professional endeavors. Our husbands, Ray and Andy, along with our families, continue to offer emotional and psychological support.

benefits from entering competitions

There are many positive benefits from entering competitions, such as the following:

- ➢ Competitions provide opportunities for growth and development of specific skills, including
  - ○ creative problem solving,
  - ○ critical thinking,
  - ○ leadership,
  - ○ group dynamics, and
  - ○ communication.

- ➢ Competitions build self-confidence, especially as you have the chance to feel a sense of satisfaction from accomplishments.
- ➢ Competitions serve as vehicles for self-directed learning, which makes you more responsible in planning and carrying out your goals.
- ➢ Some competitions offer opportunities for cooperative-learning experiences, when you work with teams or groups of students.
- ➢ Competitions serve as outlets for displaying a variety of great products, including experiments, paintings, essays, films, inventions, photographs, songs, posters, or even sculptures.
- ➢ Competitions challenge you.
- ➢ Competitions improve your personal skills, including
  - ○ time management,
  - ○ punctuality,
  - ○ following directions,
  - ○ meeting and greeting new and different people, and
  - ○ responsibility and planning.

- ➢ Competitions are a constructive use of your time.
- ➢ Competitions give you a chance to experiment with some new and different "tools" for expressing yourself and your ideas.

- ➢ Competitions enhance your interests, giving you an opportunity to build on your current interests and attain new ones.
- ➢ Competitions give you a chance to meet many new people. Not only will you make new friends as you meet other students your age, but you will also meet many adult mentors who work in a variety of fields. Competitions serve as great networking tools.
- ➢ Competitions are a way of being recognized for your strengths, abilities, and interests.
- ➢ Competitions offer tangible awards such as scholarships, cash prizes, trophies, ribbons, certificates, travel, or other fun prizes.

selecting a competition

As you go through this book and think about competitions that interest you, you'll have to make some decisions. Deciding which competitions best suit you is probably the most important one. Use the following steps to help you select a competition that will enhance your strengths and abilities.

- ➢ Assess your talent area. Ask yourself, "What talents do I have?" List the areas in which you do very well. These may include math, science, history, reading, drawing, creative writing, web design, blogging, singing, playing the piano, photography, or leadership.
- ➢ List your interests.
- ➢ List things you would like to learn more about or areas you would like to improve.
- ➢ Combine these lists. Rank order the items and select the top five areas.
- ➢ Select several competitions that may help you improve and build on your strengths and interests.
- ➢ Read the description for each competition. Ask yourself the following questions:

- ○ Can I do what is expected?
- ○ Is this competition in my area of ability and/or interest?
- ○ Do I have time to participate?
- ○ Do I have the resources needed for participation?
- ○ Will I need a sponsor? If so, can I get one? How can I get one?
- ○ If a team is needed, are there other students interested?
- ○ Is my idea practical and original?

- ➤ Discuss your ideas with a teacher, your parents, and friends. Seek their advice. They may give you some really good ideas, but remember, they may not tell you what you want to hear. Take the suggestions that are good for you and keep working toward your goal.
- ➤ Talk to other students who have participated in the competition you selected (or one similar to it). Ask them about their experiences.
- ➤ Brainstorm and write down the positive and negative aspects of entering the competition.
- ➤ Be sure to check your calendar.
- ➤ Select a competition based upon this assessment and have a fantastic time preparing for and participating in it.
- ➤ Evaluate yourself and the competition. Reflect on the experience, celebrate your efforts, and set new goals for future competitions.

things to keep in mind

Competing in competitions can be positive or negative experiences, depending on why you want to be involved. Being in a contest can help you improve and achieve, not only in the area of the competition, but also in interpersonal and personal skills. You will discover a new sense of motivation, energy, and self-confidence to improve, persevere, and excel. You will be able to gauge your own abilities against those of others. As you do so, you will find yourself working harder toward reaching your goals.

In setting your competition goals, plan to become involved only in those competitions for which you have the time, abilities, and interests. Set your own priorities and stick to them. Keep yourself balanced and don't overload yourself with too many competitive events.

Over competitiveness can lead to some possible pitfalls. Some people may let their personal values and ethics go by the wayside and do improper things just to win. Too much rivalry may result in hurt feelings among friends. You may put yourself under too much pressure and set yourself up for feelings of failure. Keep your sense of humor, and if you are feeling stressed out, always remember that good health and exercise have been shown to help relieve stress and anxiety.

One major stress factor in becoming involved in competitions is the possibility of winning or losing. What if you don't win? Of course, you will be disappointed and unhappy. It is only natural to feel that way. But remember: Competitions are learning experiences in themselves. Consider all the knowledge you'll obtain, the friends you'll make, and the opportunities you'll experience.

You can also think about what you did and how you can improve. It often helps to record your ideas in a Competitions Journal. After the competition, ask yourself the following questions:

> What did I learn?
> What did I do right?
> What could I have done better?
> What do I need to do in order to do better in the future?

After examining your answers to these questions, you will want to get involved in competitions again. Feel good about yourself. Strive for improving yourself and becoming the best possible. Most importantly, remember to have fun doing it.

members only

There are several organizations, associations, and clubs that have competitions for members only. Usually, a membership fee and active group participation are required. You may already belong to one or more of these through your school or community involvement. If you would like more information, there are a couple of ways to get it. Look online or in your local telephone directory to see if there is a local group, or ask your school counselor or principal if your school already has one. Another way to find what you need to know is to write directly to the organization or visit its website. Listed below is a sampling of organizations, clubs, and associations that require membership.

American Morgan Horse
Association
4066 Shelburne Road, Suite 5
Shelburne, VT 05482-6908
http://www.morganhorse.com

Boys and Girls Clubs of America
1275 Peachtree Street NE
Atlanta, GA 30309-3506
http://www.bgca.org

Boy Scouts of America
National Council
P.O. Box 152079
Irving, TX 75015-2079
http://www.scouting.org

Business Professionals of
America
5454 Cleveland Avenue
Columbus, OH 43231-4021
http://www.bpa.org

DECA
1908 Association Drive
Reston, VA 20191
http://www.deca.org

Future Business Leaders of
America-Phi Beta Lambda
1912 Association Drive
Reston, VA 20191-1591
http://www.fbla-pbl.org

Girls Inc.
120 Wall Street
New York, NY 10005-3902
http://www.girlsinc.org

Girl Scouts of the United States
of America
420 Fifth Avenue
New York, NY 10018-2798
http://www.girlscouts.org

HOSA-Future Health
Professionals
548 Silicon Drive, Suite 101
Southlake, TX 76092
http://www.hosa.org

Key Club International
3636 Woodview Trace
Indianapolis, IN 46268
http://www.keyclub.org

National Beta Club
151 Beta Club Way
Spartanburg, SC 29306-3012
http://www.betaclub.org

National Forensic League
125 Watson Street
P.O. Box 38
Ripon, WI 54971-0038
http://www.
nationalforensicleague.org/

National Future Farmers of
America Organization
P.O. Box 68960
6060 FFA Dr.
Indianapolis, IN 46268-0960
http://www.ffa.org

National Junior Classical League
422 Wells Mill Drive
Miami University
Oxford, OH 45056
http://www.njcl.org

National Junior Horticultural
Association
15 Railroad Avenue
Homer City, PA 15748-1378
http://www.njha.org

National Scholastic Press
Association
2221 University Avenue SE,
Suite 121
Minneapolis, MN 55414
http://www.studentpress.org/
nspa

National Management
Association
2210 Arbor Boulevard
Dayton, OH 45439
http://www.nma1.org

Quill and Scroll International
Honorary Society
100 Adler Journalism Building
Iowa City, IA 52242
http://www.quillandscroll.org

Technology Student Association
1914 Association Drive
Reston, VA 20191-1540
http://www.tsaweb.org

United States Chess Federation
P.O. Box 3967
Crossville, TN 38557
http://www.uschess.org

PART I
LIST OF COMPETITIONS

Competition	**American Association of Teachers of Spanish and Portuguese (AATSP) Poster Contest**
Sponsor	The American Association of Teachers of Spanish and Portuguese 900 Ladd Road Walled Lake, MI 48390
Web Address	http://www.aatsp.org
Areas	Foreign language and visual arts
Competition Origin	Mid-1980s
Purpose	For students of Spanish or Portuguese to express their ideas and understandings of language and culture through drawing.
Description	Entries must be 12" x 18" and may be drawn in markers (preferred) or paint. They may include captions in Spanish and/or Portuguese. Visit the website for guidelines and an application.
Eligibility	Students in grades K–12. There are four grade divisions: K–3, 4–5, 6–8, and 9–12.
Important Dates	Entries are due in early April. See guidelines for specific dates.
How to Enter	Students must be sponsored by a teacher who is a member of AATSP. Submissions need to be made following the application guidelines on the website.
Judging Criteria	Applicability to the annual theme, uniqueness, and creativity.
Judges	Members of the AATSP Poster Contest Committee.
Winner Notification	Winners are notified by the end of May.
Awards	Prizes will be awarded for the first-, second-, and third-place winners in each of the grade categories. Each entry will also receive a poster contest certificate suitable for framing.

Competition	**Academic Games Leagues of America National Tournament**
Sponsor	Academic Games Leagues of America, Inc. (AGLOA) P.O. Box 17563 West Palm Beach, FL 33416
Web Address	http://agloa.org/
Areas	Language arts, mathematics, and social studies
Competition Origin	1966
Purpose	To challenge capable students in mathematics, social studies, and language arts, and to provide recognition for these outstanding students.
Description	National tournaments are held in eight states annually. Players compete in four divisions comprised of eight logic-based games using either a board game format or answering oral questions.
Eligibility	Students in grades 4–12. There are four grade divisions: Elementary (4–6), Middle (7–8), Junior (9–10), and Senior (11–12).
Important Dates	Registration deadlines begin in January. The national tournament is held in April each year. See guidelines for specific dates.
How to Enter	Contact a local league or visit the website.
Judging Criteria	In accordance with each game's rules.
Judges	Judging is conducted by local teachers and officials. Judging assistance is provided for new programs.
Winner Notification	Winners are notified at the site of each tournament.
Awards	Local league awards are arranged from local sponsors. National tournament awards and scholarships are presented on site and vary yearly.
Advice	These competitions foster the same type of team camaraderie as most sports teams. Students are challenged to apply their knowledge and skills. Information about each game's rules and purposes are located on the website.

Competition	Achievement Awards in Writing
Sponsor	National Council of Teachers of English 1111 W. Kenyon Road Urbana, IL 61801-1096
Web Address	http://www.ncte.org
Area	Language arts
Competition Origin	1957
Purpose	To encourage high school juniors in their writing and to recognize publicly some of the best student writers in the nation.
Description	Students submit two pieces of original writing: themed and best. The themed writing must be in prose; the best writing may be in any genre (poetry, narrative, argument, expository). Contact the sponsor for a brochure or visit the website for more details.
Eligibility	Students in grade 11.
Important Dates	Entries are accepted online from late November until mid-February.
How to Enter	Students must be nominated for entry by their school's English department, which should coordinate all student entries. The number of entries allotted to the school is dependent upon the number of students enrolled in 10th, 11th, and 12th grades.
Judging Criteria	Best and themed writings are judged as a whole on content, purpose, audience, tone, word choice, organization, development, and style.
Judges	Teams of judges consisting of high school and college English teachers.
Winner Notification	Winners are notified in May.
Awards	Each winner receives a letter and certificate.
Advice	Tenth graders with outstanding writing skills should contact 11th-grade English teachers now.

Competition	**ACL/NJCL National Greek Examination**
Sponsor	The American Classical League Miami University 422 Wells Mill Drive Oxford, OH 45056
Web Address	http://aclclassics.org
Area	Foreign language
Competition Origin	1980
Purpose	To provide first-, second-, and third-year high school and college students of Attic or Homeric Greek with an examination by which they can measure their achievement against that of students in other schools.
Description	The usual sequence of exams is Introduction to Greek, Beginning Attic, Intermediate Attic, Attic Prose, and Attic Tragedy. Students take the exam that most closely matches their experience. Each examination lasts 50 minutes and contains 40 questions with multiple-choice answers. Guidelines and syllabi may be obtained by writing to the sponsor.
Eligibility	Students in grades 9–12 and college.
Important Dates	Applications must be submitted by mid-January, and the examinations are mailed out at the end of February. See guidelines for specific dates.
How to Enter	Contact your school guidance counselor, principal, or teacher.
Judging Criteria	Accuracy of answers.
Judges	The exams are graded by computer.
Winner Notification	Winners are notified upon completion of grading, typically at the end of April.
Awards	Winners receive purple, blue, red, or green ribbons and hand-lettered certificates, which are mailed to the Greek teacher at each participating school during the last 2 weeks of April. A typed list with the names of all the winners, their ranks, and schools is mailed at the same time. Winners are also announced on the website. Seniors who are purple or blue ribbon winners may apply for a $1,000 scholarship.

15

Advice A packet of previous exams can be obtained from the sponsor for a small fee. Applications for this contest are only accepted from teachers, and entrants pay a fee for each exam.

Competition	**American Association of Teachers of French (AATF) National French Contest**
Sponsor	American Association of Teachers of French (AATF) P.O. Box 3283 St Charles, IL 60174-3283
Web Address	http://www.frenchteachers.org/concours
Area	Foreign language
Competition Origin	1993
Purpose	To motivate students in teaching and learning French.
Description	Students take a 60-minute exam constructed by the American Association of Teachers of French. Guidelines may be obtained on the website or by writing to the sponsor.
Eligibility	Students of French in grades 1–12.
Important Dates	Dates vary in February and March according to each grade level. See guidelines for specific dates.
How to Enter	French teachers must enter students. The teachers will have to contact their local contest administrator, who can be found through the website or by contacting the sponsor.
Judging Criteria	Accuracy of answers.
Judges	AATF computer scoring.
Winner Notification	Winners are notified in a "timely fashion."
Awards	There are two categories of awards: chapter and national. Chapters offer prizes to those students who are among the top scorers at the chapter level for each level and division. National prizes are subsidized out of the fees paid by each entrant. Prizes awarded by Le Grand Concours include medals and certificates. National winners are students who earn the top ten scores.
Advice	It is a good idea for teachers to enter all of their students in the contest, not just potential winners. There is a small fee for each test (less than $5).

Competition	**American Association of Teachers of German (AATG) National German Exam**
Sponsor	American Association of Teachers of German, Inc. 112 Haddontowne Court #104 Cherry Hill, NJ 08034-3668
Web Address	http://www.aatg.org/NGE
Area	Foreign language
Competition Origin	1970
Purpose	To increase student interest in proficiency in German.
Description	Students are administered the AATG test in their schools. Write for guidelines in September or visit the website year-round.
Eligibility	Students who are enrolled in second-, third-, or fourth-year German classes. Those scoring at or above the 90th percentile are eligible to apply for a study trip to Germany (if applicable).
Important Dates	The exam period is from December to February.
How to Enter	Contact the German teacher in the local high school.
Judging Criteria	Accuracy of answers.
Judges	Testing committee.
Winner Notification	Winners are notified in March.
Awards	Many chapters honor students at awards ceremonies, luncheons, and dinners with prizes, including certificates for placing at the 70th percentile and above, books, special medals, T-shirts, savings bonds, and cash. In the past, study trips have been awarded to students selected by a national committee.
Advice	Teachers should enroll all students of German in the competition.

Competition	**American Computer Science League (ACSL) Competitions**
Sponsor	American Computer Science League 10 Brisas Drive West Warwick, RI 02893
Web Address	http://www.acsl.org
Area	Technology
Competition Origin	1979
Purpose	To provide a unique and exciting educational opportunity for computer enthusiasts. Contest problems motivate students to study computer topics not covered in their school's curricula and to pursue classroom topics in-depth.
Description	Contests are held at each participating school, and an unlimited number of students may compete. A school's score is the sum of the scores of its three or five highest scoring students. In each competition, students are given short theoretical and applied questions, and then a practical problem to solve within the following 3 days, testing it on data using their school's computer facilities. After the contest is administered by the faculty advisor, each school's results are returned to ACSL for tabulation. At the end of the year, an Invitational Team All-Star Contest is held at a common site. The Classroom Division consists of only pencil-and-paper questions; there are no programming problems. This division is open to all students from all grades not competing in any other division. Guidelines may be obtained on the website or by writing to the sponsor.
Eligibility	Students in grades 6–12. There are four divisions: Classroom Division (all grades); Junior Division (junior high and middle school students with no previous experience); Intermediate Division (non-experienced high school students and advanced junior high students); and Senior Division (experienced high school students).
Important Dates	Schools begin registering in July. Contests are administered in December, February, March, and April. See guidelines for specific dates.

Judging Criteria	Accuracy of answers.
Judges	Local schools score results.
Winner Notification	The All-Star Team is announced in May.
Awards	The top scoring team and the top scoring student in each geographic region within each of the League's divisions are awarded trophies. An award ribbon is given to each school for presentation to that school's top scoring student. The students on each of the top scoring teams in each division are awarded a trophy. The two top scoring schools in each division are each presented with a technological gadget, like a Kindle Touch.
Advice	Awards may vary due to changes in sponsorship and resources each year. There are sample problems and solutions on the website.

Competition	**American Foreign Service Association National High School Essay Contest**
Sponsor	American Foreign Service Association 2101 E Street NW Washington, DC 20037
Web Address	http://www.afsa.org/essay_contest.aspx
Areas	Language arts, leadership
Competition Origin	1999
Purpose	Exploring the role diplomacy has in U.S. relations with foreign countries.
Description	This is an essay competition based on a yearly topic about ambassadors to foreign countries and their role in foreign relations.
Eligibility	High school students in grades 9–12 whose parents are not in the American Foreign Service.
Important Dates	April 15 is the deadline for submissions.
How to Enter	Write an essay on the current year topic of not more than 1250 words. All entries must be submitted in Microsoft word format. For a full list of rules and regulations visit the website, where there is also a registration form available.
Judging Criteria	Writing skills and relevance to the current topic.
Judges	Judges will be skilled in writing and diplomacy.
Winner Notification	Winners are notified by June.
Awards	The winning essay receives $2,500, an all-expense paid trip to Washington, DC, and the opportunity to meet with the U.S. Secretary of State.
Advice	Check website for current year's topic and revisions in deadlines.

Competition	**American High School Theatre Festival**
Sponsor	American High School Theatre Festival 218 West Water Street, Suite 400 Charlottesville, VA 22902
Web Address	http://www.ahstf.org
Area	Performing arts
Competition Origin	1994
Purpose	To complement high school drama programs and allow the nation's drama students to showcase their skills within an international forum.
Description	Selected schools attend the Edinburgh Fringe Festival, the world's largest performing arts festival. Guidelines may be obtained on the website or by writing to the sponsor.
Eligibility	High school theatre groups are eligible for nomination. Nominations may only be submitted by college or university professors; state, regional, or national theatre organization or association members; or past alumni (winning teachers) of AHSTF.
Important Dates	Nominations must be received by mid-December. Applications for nominees are due online in early February. See the website for specific dates.
How to Enter	Nominations may be submitted online at the website.
Judging Criteria	Top high school programs are selected based upon their most recent bodies of work, awards, community involvement, philosophies, and recommendations.
Judges	Each nominated school receives an application, and all completed applications are reviewed by the AHSTF Board of Advisors. The panel of college theatre professionals comes from all corners of the country.
Winner Notification	Selected schools are notified by August.
Awards	Round-trip airfare to London; guided tour of London; two nights' London accommodation; West End theatre performance; private chartered train from London to Edinburgh; tube/bus half-day guided sightseeing in Edinburgh and full-day countryside trip on chartered motor coaches; four performance

slots at AHSTF's international venue; two meals daily; 10 nights accommodations in Edinburgh; AHSTF welcome reception and post-program awards ceremony; and admission to Military Tattoo on the grounds of the Edinburgh Castle.

Advice

Self-nominations are not accepted.

Competition	**American History Essay Contest**
Sponsor	National Society Daughters of the American Revolution 1776 D St. NW Washington, DC 20006-5303
Web Address	http://www.dar.org/natsociety
Areas	Social studies and language arts
Competition Origin	1966
Purpose	To encourage young people to think creatively about the history of our nation and to learn about history in a new light.
Description	A selected essay topic for use during the academic year is announced, and contest instructions are sent to the schools by participating chapters on a yearly basis. Information can be obtained through the DAR state chairperson in your state.
Eligibility	Students in grades 5–8.
Important Dates	Contact your local chapter or visit the website for deadlines.
How to Enter	Contact the DAR chapter of the state in which the student resides.
Judging Criteria	Essays are judged for historical accuracy, adherence to topic, organization of materials, interest, originality, spelling, grammar, punctuation, and neatness.
Judges	State-level judging is determined by each chapter; judging at the national level is supervised by the DAR National Society. The winning essay from each of the four grades on the regional level will be judged on the national level.
Winner Notification	Winners are notified after the national-level judging is complete.
Awards	Each student participant receives a certificate of participation from the chapter, and the chapter winners receive bronze medals and certificates. State winners receive certificates and silver medals. National winners receive special certificates, medals, and a monetary award.

Competition	**American Mathematics Competitions (AMC)**
Sponsor	The Mathematical Association of America 1529 18th Street NW Washington, DC 20036-1358
Web Address	http://amc.maa.org
Area	Mathematics
Competition Origin	1950
Purpose	To provide a friendly challenge to students, as well as an opportunity to recognize mathematical talent.
Description	National contests called the American Mathematics Contest 8 (AMC 8); the American Mathematics Contest 10 (AMC 10); the American Mathematics Contest 12 (AMC 12); the American Invitational Mathematics Examination (AIME); the United States of America Mathematical Olympiad (USAMO); the United States of America Junior Mathematical Olympiad (USAJMO); Mathematical Olympiad Summer Program (MOSP) and International Mathematical Olympiad (IMO) are held each year. Contests consist of multiple-choice or essay/proof tests of mathematics. Guidelines are available early in the school year.
Eligibility	Students in grades 6–12.
Important Dates	Dates vary with each contest. See the webpage for a calendar of specific dates for all competitions.
How to Enter	Contact the sponsor.
Judging Criteria	Accuracy of answers.
Judges	Tests are scored electronically.
Winner Notification	Winners are notified upon receipt and scoring of exams.
Awards	Awards vary but as winners move through the contests, the top 230 AMC winners move into the USAMO, competing for the top twelve spaces, which are honored at an awards ceremony in Washington, DC. Six of these students represent the US in the International Mathematical Olympiad.

Competition	**American Regions Mathematics League Competition**
Sponsor	American Regions Mathematics League
Web Address	http://arml.com
Area	Mathematics
Competition Origin	1976
Purpose	To make students more comfortable with their abilities and introduce them to new and exciting areas of math.
Description	The annual competition is designed for both teams and individuals on the teams. The Team Round consists of short-answer questions the team members work on cooperatively. The Power Round forces the team to use various methods of mathematical analysis and proof; members must then expand and generalize from the topic. The conclusions are put together in the form of a report. The Individual Round allows participants to work independently on several questions within a mandated time frame. The Relay Round sets up "subteams" within a team: The answer to one team member's question is used by another to answer the next. Credit is given only if the final team member answers correctly. Guidelines may be obtained on the website.
Eligibility	Students in grades 6–12 (the contest is written for high school students, but exceptional junior high students can compete).
Important Dates	See guidelines for specific dates.
How to Enter	Registration forms are available on the website.
Judging Criteria	Varies with each competition. Accuracy of answers is the key factor.
Judges	American Regions Mathematics League officials and volunteers.
Winner Notification	Winners are notified at each stage of competition.
Awards	All participants receive a certificate for participation. Other prizes include trophies and plaques.
Advice	Previous years' exams are available online.

Competition	**American Scholastic Mathematics Association Annual Mathematics Contest**
Sponsor	American Scholastic Mathematics Association PO Box 564400 College Point, NY 11356-4400
Web Address	http://www.asan.com/asma1.htm
Area	Mathematics
Competition Origin	2004
Purpose	To promote excellence in mathematics skills.
Description	Each team must have 8 members with 2 alternates and will answer 7 math problems in a 35-minute time limit.
Eligibility	Students in grades 7–12, with a senior division and a junior division.
Important Dates	Deadline for entry is July 1.
How to Enter	Entry form and rules are available on the website.
Judging Criteria	Highest scoring team will be declared the winner.
Judges	Judges will be knowledgeable in mathematics.
Winner Notification	Winners will be announced in the Final Awards Newsletter.
Awards	Certificates will be awarded to winning teams.
Advice	Check the website for updates to deadlines and information regarding types of questions to expect.

Competition	**AMVETS Americanism Program**
Sponsor	AMVETS and AMVETS Auxiliary Program National Headquarters 4647 Forbes Blvd. Lanham, MD 20706
Web Address	http://www.amvets.org
Areas	Language arts, social studies, and visual arts
Competition Origin	1950s
Purpose	To promote Americanism through drawing and essay writing.
Description	This patriotic program helps teach students about their American heritage, civics, and citizenship. Students design flags or posters and write essays.
Eligibility	Students in grades K–12. There are three grade divisions: Flag Drawing (K–1); Poster Contest (2–5); and Essay Writing (6–12).
Important Dates	Local entries are due to local AMVETS departments at least 30 days before the national deadline of 1 July, where they are judged and submitted for national consideration.
How to Enter	Applications are available online and from local sponsors.
Judging Criteria	Entries are judged on originality, adherence to theme, and literary composition or artistic ability.
Judges	Local and national judges appointed by AMVETS.
Winner Notification	Varies with local contest dates.
Awards	Winners receive gift cards valued at up to $150 for the poster and flag design contests and $500 for the essay contest. All ninth-grade first-place winners receive a trip to Valley Forge for a long weekend of youth activities with dynamic speakers and sightseeing.

Competition	**Ayn Rand Novels Essay Contests**
Sponsor	The Ayn Rand Institute 2121 Alton Parkway, Suite 250 Irvine, CA 92606-4926
Web Address	http://aynrandnovels.org/essay-contests.html
Area	Language arts
Competition Origin	1985
Purpose	To promote awareness of Ayn Rand's works and philosophy, and to encourage writing among junior and high school students.
Description	The essay contest consists of four categories with three topics to choose from in each category. Each category is age specific and has its own guidelines.
Eligibility	Students in grades 8–12.
Important Dates	Deadlines are in March, April, or May depending on the category entered.
How to Enter	Entries can be electronically delivered or mailed. See the website for specific entry rules and deadlines.
Judging Criteria	Based on style and content.
Judges	Judges are chosen for their knowledge in writing skills and styles.
Winner Notification	Winners will be notified via e-mail or U.S. mail.
Awards	1st place ranges from $2,000 to $10,000 depending on the category entered. Varying cash prizes are awarded to 2nd place, 3rd place, finalist, and semifinalists.
Advice	Check website for available category subjects.

Competition	**Annual Math League Contests**
Sponsor	Mathematics Leagues
Web Address	http://www.mathleague.com
Area	Mathematics
Competition Origin	1977
Purpose	To encourage student interest and confidence in mathematics through problem-solving activities.
Description	Mathematic contests comprised of timed multiple-choice tests. Guidelines are posted throughout the year and may be obtained through the website.
Eligibility	Students in grades 4–12.
Important Dates	Dates will vary for each grade level. See guidelines for specific dates.
How to Enter	You may register through the website. You may also print an order form from the website and mail it to the sponsor.
Judging Criteria	Accuracy of answers.
Judges	The contest is scored by machines.
Winner Notification	Varies with competition deadlines.
Awards	Certificates for high scorers and certificates of achievement are awarded.
Advice	Sample tests are on the website.

Competition	**Beneath the Sea's Ocean Pals Poster Contest**
Sponsor	Beneath the Sea, Inc. 495 New Rochelle Road, Ste. 2A Bronxville, NY 10708
Web Address	http://www.beneaththesea.org
Areas	Visual arts and science
Competition Origin	1986
Purpose	To encourage students to become aware of marine environments.
Description	Students make posters depicting the current year's theme on protecting marine environments. Current theme can be found on website.
Eligibility	Students in grades K–12, with four age categories. International students may apply to the international version of this contest.
Important Dates	Deadline for entry is in December.
How to Enter	Posters must be drawn or painted freehand on standard poster board using pens, pencils, colored pencils, markers or crayons, watercolors, or acrylic paints. Current theme must be incorporated in the poster as a slogan or wording.
Judging Criteria	Creativity, originality, and incorporation of the current theme.
Judges	A panel of independent judges recognized for their work in marine art, marine environment, or art education will be assembled to view and select winners.
Winner Notification	Winners will be notified in writing and will be announced at the Beneath the Sea Expo.
Awards	1st–3rd place regional winners, by division, receive medals and $50–$100 U.S. savings bonds. 1st–3rd place national winners, by division, receive $75–$200 U.S. savings bonds. One national 1st-place winner will win a trip to the Cayman Islands. International winners receive a medal and a $100 gift check.
Advice	Check website for current theme and deadlines. Read all rules and regulations posted on the website. Be sure to check for which regional address you should send your application to when you apply.

Competition	**Beneath the Sea's Ocean Pals Digital Imaging Contest**
Sponsor	Beneath the Sea, Inc. 495 New Rochelle Road, Ste. 2A Bronxville, NY 10708
Web Address	http://www.beneaththesea.org
Areas	Visual arts and science
Competition Origin	1986
Purpose	To encourage students to become aware of marine environments.
Description	Students submit digital photos of water-related images.
Eligibility	Students in K–12, with four age categories.
Important Dates	Deadline for entry is in December.
How to Enter	Send digital photos from a point and shoot camera that have not been enhanced on a CD along with the entry form that is available on the website to Beneath the Sea – Ocean Pals Photo Contest, 495 New Rochelle Road – Suite 2A, Bronxville, NY 10708.
Judging Criteria	Creativity, originality, and incorporation of the current theme.
Judges	Members of Beneath the Sea's Ocean Pals along with a team of professional photo judges will judge this digital image contest.
Winner Notification	Winners will be notified in writing and will be announced at the Beneath the Sea Expo.
Awards	1st place in each division will receive a medal and $100 gift check.
Advice	Check website for deadlines. Read all rules and regulations posted on the website.

Competition	**BEST Robotics**
Sponsor	BEST Robotics, Inc. P.O. Box 1024 Georgetown, TX 78627
Web Address	http://www.bestinc.org
Areas	Engineering, mathematics, science, and technology
Competition Origin	1994
Purpose	To promote teamwork, problem solving, project management, and pride.
Description	In a 6-week period students have to create a radio-controlled robot along with a project notebook, oral presentation, and an interview. Each student also works with teams ranging anywhere from 5–60 students. The guidelines can be obtained by contacting the local sponsor by e-mail or through the website.
Eligibility	Students in grades 6–12.
Important Dates	The regional competitions are held in December, with the national championship in April. See guidelines for specific dates.
How to Enter	Participants may register online through the website.
Judging Criteria	Students are judged on creativity, the use of technology, publicity, presentation, participation, enthusiasm, sportsmanship, and robot performance.
Judges	Engineers and other technical professionals.
Winner Notification	Winners are notified at local and regional tournament sites.
Awards	First-, second-, and third-place awards are given along with several other special awards such as the BEST Award, Competition Award, Founders Award for Creative Design, Most Robust, Most Elegant, Most Photogenic, T-Shirt Award, and Webpage Award.
Advice	Anyone—colleges/universities, corporations, individuals—can start a new hub serving a minimum of eight teams. Local hubs rely on financial support from corporations and/or colleges/universities in order to allow schools to participate at no cost.

Competition	**The Blank Theatre Young Playwrights Competition & Festival**
Sponsor	The Blank Theatre P.O. Box 38756 Hollywood, CA 90038
Web Address	http://www.youngplaywrights.com
Areas	Language arts and performing arts
Competition Origin	1993
Purpose	To develop and produce plays and musicals by playwrights 19 years of age and younger.
Description	Students submit up to three original plays or musicals. Plays can be cowritten, provided none of the writers are older than 19 years old. Winning plays will be performed.
Eligibility	Students ages 19 and younger (as of deadline).
Important Dates	The deadline for entry is March 15. Winning plays are performed at the festival in June.
How to Enter	Review the formatting and submission guidelines (see the website) and submit an original script that adheres to these guidelines. All submissions must include a cover sheet. Submissions can be made by mail or e-mail (PDF format).
Judging Criteria	Selections are based on the quality of writing in playwriting competition.
Judges	Judges are theater professionals.
Winner Notification	Winners will be notified in May.
Awards	Production of the play in the Young Playwrights Festival. Authors participate in casting and rehearsal of their plays, which are then performed by professional actors.

Competition	**BOOK IT! National Reading Incentive Program**
Sponsor	Pizza Hut, BOOK IT! P.O. Box 2999 Wichita, KS 67201
Web Address	http://www.bookitprogram.com
Area	Language arts
Competition Origin	1985
Purpose	To develop a lifelong love of reading in children.
Description	Students in participating classes meet reading goals as established by the classroom teacher to win prizes. Teachers can request guidelines from the sponsor year-round, and they are also available on the website.
Eligibility	Students in grades K–6.
Important Dates	The program usually begins in early October and runs through the end of March. See guidelines for specific dates.
How to Enter	Talk to your classroom teacher or principal.
Judging Criteria	Teachers set monthly reading goals, which may vary from month to month. Goals may include the numbers of books read, number of pages or chapters read, number of minutes spent reading, and so forth.
Judges	Classroom teacher sets the goals.
Winner Notification	Everyone wins. Each classroom teacher may handle awards differently.
Awards	There are a variety of awards given such as posters, cutouts, fun reading activities, family involvement, and pizza awards.
Advice	Be sure to discuss this early with your teacher or school principal.

Competition	**Botball Robotics**
Sponsor	KISS Institute for Practical Robotics 1818 W. Lindsey, Bldg. D, Ste. 100 Norman, OK 73069
Web Address	http://www.botball.org
Areas	Engineering, mathematics, science, and technology
Competition Origin	2000
Purpose	To promote hands-on experience in science, technology, engineering, and math.
Description	Students in 5–10-member teams design, build, and program a robot. The website has all the information needed to join or start a team.
Eligibility	Students in grades 6–12.
Important Dates	Schools should register by early January to receive a discount; otherwise, register 2 weeks prior to your regional tournament. Botball regional tournaments are held March through May. See guidelines for specific dates.
How to Enter	Students may register online through the website.
Judging Criteria	Students are judged according to use of robotics equipment, attendance during teacher tutorials, number of students participating, and future plans for funding of the robot.
Judges	Volunteers, sponsors, and mentors in each region.
Winner Notification	Winners are announced at each tournament.
Awards	Various awards and scholarships are given to the winners of this competition, dependent upon region and sponsorship.
Advice	This is an expensive, team-based competition. Visit the website to find out if there is a team in your area.

Competition	**Bridge Building Contest**
Sponsor	Institute of Technology Office of Undergraduate Admissions, and the Illinois Engineering Council
Web Address	http://bridgecontest.phys.iit.edu/
Areas	Engineering and technology
Competition Origin	1997
Purpose	To construct model bridges based on real-life bridges.
Description	This bridge building competition is reliant on constructing bridges that can carry the most loads. To be eligible for the international competition students must compete in a regional competition. Guidelines for establishing a regional competition are on the website.
Eligibility	High school students are eligible to compete.
Important Dates	International competition date is determined on a year-to-year basis.
How to Enter	Bridges must be constructed of basswood and cannot exceed 25 grams. Wood cannot be painted, stained, or coated with any material. For complete rules, see the website.
Judging Criteria	The bridge with the highest structural efficiency will be declared the winner.
Judges	A panel of judges knowledgeable in bridge building will judge the entries.
Winner Notification	Winners are announced at the conclusion of the competition and listed online.
Awards	Winner of the international competition will receive a one-half tuition scholarship to Illinois Institute of Technology.
Advice	Those interested in participating should check the website for information on date and location of current competition.

Competition	**Christopher Columbus Awards**
Sponsor	The Christopher Columbus Awards 105 Terry Drive, Ste. 120 Newtown, PA 18940
Web Address	http://www.christophercolumbusawards.com
Areas	Creativity/problem solving, science, service learning, and technology
Competition Origin	1996
Purpose	To encourage students' curiosity and creativity in order to help them improve their community through scientific and technological innovation.
Description	Students compete in groups of three to four people with an adult coach. The teams have to identify a problem in their community and create a solution. Guidelines can be obtained through the website.
Eligibility	Students in grades 6–8.
Important Dates	The deadline for entry is early February. See guidelines for specific dates.
How to Enter	Registration forms are online.
Judging Criteria	Students are judged on their creativity, innovation, scientific accuracy, feasibility, and communication.
Judges	The sponsor selects judges from the fields of science and technology.
Winner Notification	Winners are notified in mid-April.
Awards	Every team that enters receives a certificate and judges' comments. Thirty semifinalist teams receive a T-shirt and certificate of participation. Eight finalist teams receive an all-expenses-paid trip to Walt Disney World and a $200 developmental grant. The two gold medal teams receive a $2,000 cash prize and a medal for each team member and the sponsoring school. The winning team receives a $25,000 grant.
Advice	Competition guides for coaches and students can be downloaded from the website.

Competition	**Civil Rights Defense Fund Youth Essay Contest**
Sponsor	The National Rifle Association of America NRA Civil Rights Defense Fund 11250 Waples Mill Road Fairfax, VA 22030
Web Address	http://www.nradefensefund.org/contests-scholarships.aspx
Area	Social studies and language arts
Competition Origin	1978
Purpose	To celebrate the Second Amendment as an integral part of the Constitution and the Bill of Rights.
Description	Students are to write a 1,000-word essay discussing the importance of the 2nd Amendment to the United States Constitution and what it means to our country.
Eligibility	There are two age divisions, senior division grades 10–12 and junior division grades K–9.
Important Dates	Deadline for entry is in early December.
How to Enter	Submit essay in a legible format (typed and double-spaced is preferred) to the NRA Civil Rights Defense Fund. Entry form can be found on website.
Judging Criteria	Essays will be judged on originality, scholarship (including works cited), and presentation (including grammar and spelling).
Judges	Judges will be knowledgeable in writing.
Winner Notification	Winners will be notified early in the following year.
Awards	1st place in each division wins $1,000.00, 2nd place wins $600.00, 3rd place wins $200.00, and honorable mentions receive $100.00.
Advice	Check website for changes in deadlines and theme of the essay.

Competition	**Civil War Trust Essay Contest**
Sponsor	The Civil War Trust Education Department 1156 15th St. NW, Ste. 900 Washington, DC 20005
Web Address	http://www.civilwar.org/education/contests-quizzes/ essay-contest/essay-contest.html
Area	Social studies and language arts
Competition Origin	1991
Purpose	To preserve the history of the Civil War.
Description	Students compete in writing about historical events of America's Civil War. The essays should include the importance of history and the preservation of historical sites. There is a current slogan for the essay listed on the website. The competition has a senior and junior division.
Eligibility	Students in grades 4–7 are eligible for the junior division, and students from grades 8–12 are eligible for the senior division.
Important Dates	All entries must be emailed by May 1.
How to Enter	Entries should be emailed to education@civilwar.org with the subject line: "[year] Essay Contest". Use Microsoft Word or PDF format and include student name and grade, school name and address (including city, state, and zip), school phone, teacher's name, and teacher's e-mail. Essays should be around 300 words.
Judging Criteria	Judging will be based on creativity, persuasive quality, clarity, and strength of message.
Judges	Judges will be knowledgeable in English and American History.
Winner Notification	Students will be notified of the results in June. Essays will not be returned.
Awards	The senior and junior division will consist of 1st, 2nd, and 3rd place winners in each division. 1st place wins $1,000, 2nd place wins $750, and 3rd place wins $250.
Advice	Check the webpage for the current slogan and any updated information regarding deadlines.

Competition	**Civil War Trust Postcard Contest**
Sponsor	Civil War Trust Education Department 1156 15th St. NW Suite 900 Washington, DC 20005
Web Address	http://www.civilwar.org/education/contests-quizzes/ essay-contest/essay-contest.html
Area	Social studies and visual arts
Competition Origin	1991
Purpose	To preserve the history of the Civil War.
Description	Students will design an illustrated postcard using the current theme. There is a current slogan for the postcards listed on the website. The competition has a senior and junior division.
Eligibility	Students in grades 4–7 are eligible for the junior division and students from grades 8–12 are eligible for the senior division.
Important Dates	All entries must be emailed by May 1.
How to Enter	Send entries by the deadline to Civil War Trust Education Department. Post cards must be 5–6 inches long and 3.5–4.5 inches wide. The postcard should have a theme-based illustration on one side and a short note on the other side. Entries will include Student Name and Grade, School Name and Address, School City, State & Zip, School Phone, Teacher Name, and Teacher E-mail written on the postcard or stapled to the postcard.
Judging Criteria	Judging will be based on creativity, clarity, and strength of message.
Judges	Judges will be knowledgeable in art.
Winner Notification	Students will be notified of the results in June. Postcards will not be returned.
Awards	The senior and junior division will consist of 1st, 2nd, and 3rd place winners in each division. 1st place wins $1,000, 2nd place wins $750, and 3rd place wins $250.
Advice	Check the webpage for the current slogan and any updated information regarding deadlines. Previous year winners are available for viewing on the website.

Competition	**Congressional Art Competition**
Sponsor	United States House of Representatives Washington, DC 20515
Web Address	http://www.house.gov/content/educate/ art_competition/
Area	Visual arts
Competition Origin	1982
Purpose	To afford students the opportunity to express their creativity and to share these creative talents with the community.
Description	Students first submit artwork based upon a particular theme at the congressional district level, with winners moving onto compete at the national level. Contact your local congressional representative for guidelines.
Eligibility	Students in grades 9–12.
Important Dates	Congressional competitions are announced in the fall and held in the spring. See guidelines for specific dates.
How to Enter	Guidelines and entry forms are available from your local congressional representative.
Judging Criteria	Artwork is judged on creativity. All entries must be two-dimensional; no larger than 28 inches wide by 28 inches tall by 4 inches thick; not weigh more than 15 pounds; and be original in concept, design and execution.
Judges	Art and art education experts.
Winner Notification	Local dates vary, but national competition winners are notified in late spring/early summer.
Awards	All students receive a certificate signed by a member of Congress. At the district level, winning artwork is displayed for a year in local offices of Congress members. At the national level, winning artwork is displayed for a year in the Cannon Tunnel.

Competition	**Continental Mathematics League**
Sponsor	Continental Mathematics League P.O. Box 2196 St. James, NY 11780
Web Address	http://www.continentalmathematicsleague.com/
Area	Mathematics
Competition Origin	1980
Purpose	To enhance students' mathematical problem-solving skills.
Description	Meets are held throughout the year, featuring different questions per meet and division. Guidelines may be obtained on the website or by writing to the sponsor.
Eligibility	Students in grades 2–9.
Important Dates	Register by early October. Meets are held throughout the school year. See guidelines for specific dates.
How to Enter	Register by contacting the sponsor.
Judging Criteria	Accuracy of answers.
Judges	Judges are appointed for each division meet.
Winner Notification	Winners are notified in the spring.
Awards	Medals and certificates are awarded to the winners.
Advice	Check website for updates to rules and regulations as well as deadlines.

Competition	**Creative Patriotic Art Awards**
Sponsor	Ladies Auxiliary to the Veterans of Foreign Wars 406 West 34th St., 10th Floor Kansas City, MO 64111
Web Address	https://www.ladiesauxvfw.org/images/stories/PatArt2012.pdf
Area	Visual arts
Competition Origin	1979
Purpose	To show support for American troops.
Description	This is an art competition for high school students depicting a patriotic theme. All entries should be on paper or canvas.
Eligibility	Students in grades 9–12.
Important Dates	Students must submit artwork by March 31 to their local Ladies Auxiliary to the Veterans of Foreign Wars chapter.
How to Enter	Art must be on paper or canvas. Water color, pencil, pastel, charcoal, tempera, crayon, acrylic, pen-and-ink, or oil may be used. Digital art is not accepted. Do not frame. Submit canvas entries on stretcher frames. Other entries must be matted on white. Do not use other color mats. In matting, use heavy paper to reinforce back. Mounted and floating mats may also be used. The art should be no smaller than 8" x 10" but no larger than 18" x 24", not including mat. Be sure to complete entry form and attach to back of entry. (This form can be found on the website.) Note that you must be sponsored by a Ladies Auxiliary or a foreign-based Ladies Auxiliary or Post. Package art so that it can be mailed without being damaged. If you use the American Flag in your entry, it must conform to the Federal Flag Code as far as color, number of stars and stripes, and other pertinent rules of the code. Entry must have been done during the current school year—note that you must have your teacher's signature. Each student may submit only one entry.
Judging Criteria	Each entry will be judged on the originality of concept, presentation, and patriotism expressed; the content of how it relates to patriotism and clarity of

ideas; the design technique; total impact of work; and uniqueness.

Judges
Entries will be judged by teachers, professionals, and persons knowledgeable in art.

Winner Notification
Winners will be notified by mail.

Awards
First place wins $10,000; second place wins $5,000; third place wins $2,500; fourth place wins $1,500; fifth through eighth place win $500.

Advice
Check for updates and changes in deadlines.

Competition	*Cricket* **Contests**
Sponsor	The *Cricket* Magazine Group P.O. Box 300 Peru, IL 61354
Web Address	http://www.cricketmagkids.com/contests
Areas	Language arts and visual arts
Competition Origin	1973
Purpose	To encourage readers' literary and artistic creativity and to provide a forum for personal expression.
Description	Topics are drawn from issues of *Cricket* magazine. Stories, poetry, art, and photography contests are run with each issue. All work must be original, without help from anyone. Contests are found in each issue of the magazine and on its website.
Eligibility	Open to all ages, but *Cricket* magazine targets students ages 9–14.
Important Dates	This is a monthly or bi-monthly contest with entries due by the 25th of each month.
How to Enter	Entries should be mailed to *Cricket* Magazine Group.
Judging Criteria	Stories, poems, art, and photography are judged for their technique, originality, and adherence to contest themes and guidelines.
Judges	Members of *Cricket*'s editorial and art departments.
Winner Notification	Winners are notified approximately one month after entry deadline.
Awards	Eight to 15 winning entries (depending on space available) are published in two age categories (10 and under and 11 and up) three months after the issue in which the contest description appeared. The winning essays are also published on the magazine's website.
Advice	Do not e-mail or fax submissions. Only one entry per person is allowed each month.

Competition	**CyberPatriot**
Sponsor	The Air Force Association 1501 Lee Highway Arlington, VA 22209-1198
Web Address	http://www.uscyberpatriot.org/Pages/default.aspx
Area	Science, Technology, Engineering, and Mathematics
Competition Origin	2009
Purpose	To encourage students to pursue careers in cybersecurity and other STEM disciplines.
Description	Students compete in rounds, with the teams identifying the most vulnerabilities advancing to the next round for three rounds. Finalist will compete via an all-expense-paid visit to Washington, D.C.
Eligibility	Competitors must be at least 13 years old in grades 9–12 in an accredited public or private institution or a registered home school association. Teams must consist of at least two members and not more than five members. Each team must have a coach—usually a teacher or JROTC, CAP, or Sea Cadet Leader.
Important Dates	Registrations due by September 30.
How to Enter	Enter via the competition website.
Judging Criteria	The teams that discover the most vulnerabilities advance to the next round. The winners of the three rounds advance to the finals in Washington, DC.
Judges	Judges will be knowledgeable in science, math, and/or technology.
Winner Notification	Winners will be announced at the finals in Washington, DC.
Awards	Awards and scholarships are given to each of the members of the winning team.
Advice	Prior computer knowledge is not required, but there are equipment requirements.

Competition	**Destination Imagination Challenge Program**
Sponsor	Destination Imagination, Inc. 1111 South Union Avenue Cherry Hill, NJ 08002
Web Address	http://www.destinationimagination.org/what-we-do/challenge-program
Area	Creative thinking and problem solving, writing
Competition Origin	1999
Purpose	To encourage collaborative problem solving and creative thinking.
Description	Contestants choose one of seven challenges available on the website. They then write a paper explaining their solution and develop a product using those solutions.
Eligibility	Teams of up to seven members aged kindergarten through college.
Important Dates	Each season takes place from September through May.
How to Enter	Teams choose their area of focus (Technical, Scientific, Fine Arts, Improvisational, Structural and Service Learning) and develop their solutions. The teams then enter a regional competition. Winners will advance to state competitions, then national and finally global. Team registration forms can be downloaded from the website.
Judging Criteria	Winners are selected on effectiveness of solution.
Judges	The appraisers for this competition are volunteers that have been trained for the event.
Winner Notification	Winners are announced at the global competition.
Awards	Trophies and medals are awarded the winning teams.
Advice	Check website for updates and complete rules and regulations.

Competition	**Discover Card Tribute Award Scholarships**
Sponsor	American Association of School Administrators DCTA Program Coordinator P.O. Box 9338 Arlington, VA 22219
Web Address	http://www.scholarships4school.com/scholarships/discover-card-tribute-award-scholarship.html
Areas	Leadership and service learning
Competition Origin	1991
Purpose	To award scholarships in recognition of high school juniors who exhibit excellence in many areas of their lives beyond academics.
Description	Scholarships are given for education or training beyond high school. They can be used for coursework, certificate trade schools, and associate or bachelor degrees. Guidelines are available September through December of each year. Applications are sent to all schools, so check with your guidance counselor.
Eligibility	Students in grade 11 (must carry at least a 2.75 GPA during 9th and 10th grades).
Important Dates	Applications are due in early January. See guidelines for specific dates.
How to Enter	Check with your guidance counselor, write to sponsor for an application, or request one from the website above.
Judging Criteria	Tribute Award winners are selected on the basis of each student's application package. In addition to their academic achievements, winners must demonstrate outstanding accomplishments in special talents, leadership, obstacles overcome, and community service. Since all criteria areas are judged on an equal basis, winners must show outstanding accomplishments in each area. Judges are looking for the best all-around applicants.
Judges	Judging is conducted at state and national levels with representatives from business, education, and community sectors.
Winner Notification	Winners are notified in May with letters to the student, principal, and superintendent.

Awards

There are two levels of Tribute Award scholarships: State (and District of Columbia) Scholarships, which offer up to nine awards at $2,500 each, and National Scholarships, which offer up to nine awards at $25,000 each.

Competition	**Discovery Education Young Scientist Challenge**
Sponsor	Discovery Education and 3M
Web Address	http://www.youngscientistchallenge.com/
Area	Science
Competition Origin	1999
Purpose	To encourage understanding and exploration in the field of science.
Description	Students must create a 1–2 minute video describing a new innovation or solution that could solve or impact an everyday problem related to how we live, how we work, or how we play. One student will win the coveted title of "America's Top Young Scientist."
Eligibility	Students in grades 5–8.
Important Dates	Submissions are due in early June. See guidelines for specific dates.
How to Enter	Students must enter on the website.
Judging Criteria	Videos are judged based on creativity, scientific knowledge, persuasiveness and effective communication, and overall presentation.
Judges	A panel of judges from Discovery Education and its partner organizations, educators, and science professionals score each entry.
Winner Notification	Winners are notified in September.
Awards	There are up to 51 state merit prizes of approximately $299 retail value. The ten finalists participate in the Summer Mentorship Program, and receive a pocket video camera, support to create a blog, a trip to Saint Paul, Minnesota to compete in the Final Event, $1,000 cash, a medal, and the opportunity to participate in promotional events. There are also six second prizes, three runner-up prizes and a grand prize.
Advice	The website has lots of great ideas, including past winners' challenge archives. Be sure to check the website for updated information on due dates and winner notifications.

Competition	**DuPont Challenge Science Essay Awards Program**
Sponsor	DuPont Office of Education P.O. Box 80357 Wilmington, DE 19880-0030
Web Address	http://thechallenge.dupont.com/
Areas	Engineering, language arts, mathematics, and science
Competition Origin	2000
Purpose	To promote student interest in all avenues of science.
Description	The DuPont Challenge is an opportunity for students to write an essay of 700–1,000 words discussing a scientific development, event, or theory that has captured their interest and attention. Contact the sponsor for guidelines.
Eligibility	Students in grades 7–12.
Important Dates	Entries due by mid to late January. See guidelines for specific dates.
How to Enter	Complete the entry form on the website and submit it with an original essay.
Judging Criteria	An appropriate choice of subject matter; thorough research using a variety of resource materials; careful consideration of how the subject matter affects you and humankind; and a clear, well organized writing style that has been proofed for spelling and grammatical errors are judged. In a winning essay, creativity, originality, and style are important, as are a neat presentation, the quality of scientific research, good writing, and careful attention to spelling, grammar, and punctuation.
Judges	DuPont appoints judges.
Winner Notification	Winners are notified by the sponsor following competition deadlines and judging.
Awards	The program awards educational prizes totaling more than $100,000. Prizes include savings bonds, school resources, and travel. The Grand Prize Winner received an expenses-paid trip to Orlando, Florida, a $5,000 US Savings Bond, and Britannica reference materials.

Advice   Before you begin to research and write, read the
winning essays on the website and carefully review the
student competition rules.

Competition	**eCYBERMISSION**
Sponsor	U.S. Army
Web Address	http://www.ecybermission.com
Area	Mathematics, science, and technology
Competition Origin	2004
Purpose	To increase the number of students interested in science, math, and technology.
Description	Teams choose a mission, write a hypothesis, do experiments, and analyze their results. Mission folders are then submitted to the competition for judging.
Eligibility	Students in grades 6–9. Team members must be in the same grade and state. Teams must also include one adult Team Advisor over the age of 21 (see website for Team Advisor eligibility).
Important Dates	January 15 is the deadline for team entry.
How to Enter	Complete rules and regulations as well as mission choices can be viewed on the website.
Judging Criteria	Teams are judged on their use of scientific method/inquiry or engineering design process, the project's benefit to the community, and team collaboration.
Judges	Members of the U.S. Army with knowledge in math, science, and technology volunteer to evaluate and objectively score mission folders.
Winner Notification	Winners are listed on the website.
Awards	1st place national winners receive a $5,000.00 U.S. Savings Bond.
	1st place regional winners receive a $2,000.00 U.S. Savings Bond.
	1st place state winners receive a $1,000.00 U.S. Savings Bond.
	2nd place state winners receive a $500.00 U.S. Savings Bond.
Advice	Check for updates to rules, missions, and deadlines on the website.

Competition	**EGirl Essay Contest**
Sponsor	Lockheed Martin
Web Address	http://www.engineergirl.org/10209.aspx
Area	Engineering, language arts, and science
Competition Origin	2001
Purpose	To promote interest in engineering.
Description	There are three age categories for essays. Essays for grades 3–5 should be no more than 500 words, essays for grades 6–8 should have no more than 750 words, and essays for grades 9–12 should have no more than 1,500 words.
Eligibility	Students in grades 3–5 (ages 8–11), 6–8 (ages 12–14), and 9–12 (ages 15–18) can enter in their appropriate age group.
Important Dates	Deadline is March 1.
How to Enter	Submit an essay that meets the requirements of the Contest Description through the Online Submission Form located on the website for your appropriate age group.
Judging Crtieria	Essays are judged on design content, research, expression, and originality.
Judges	A panel of judges knowledgeable about the current year topics will evaluate the essays.
Winner Notification	Winners will be notified to complete publication form and will be published on the Engineer Girl website.
Awards	First-place winners will be awarded $500, second-place winners receive $250, and third-place winners receive $100.
Advice	See website for current essay topic and updates to deadlines.

Competition	**Executive Women International Scholarship Program (EWISP)**
Sponsor	Executive Women International 3860 South 2300 East Salt Lake City, UT 84109
Web Address	http://ewiconnect.com/ewiconnect/Community/EWISP_Scholarship.aspx
Area	Academic recognition
Competition Origin	1974
Purpose	To encourage, motivate, and assist high school juniors to develop career objectives and provide financial support.
Description	Students can compete at the local chapter level and at the national level. Students must complete a student application form, obtain a personal and teacher endorsement, and submit an autobiographical essay as outlined in the application. Guidelines are available through the local chapter scholarship chair. Chapter addresses and websites are located on the website.
Eligibility	Open to high school seniors.
Important Dates	Deadlines vary from chapter to chapter. See guidelines for specific dates.
How to Enter	The application form is available online. Students need a recommendation from a sponsoring teacher and community member.
Judging Criteria	Judging is based on application materials and the following criteria: scholastic achievement, extra-curricular activities, leadership qualities, and good citizenship.
Judges	Representatives of the business, education, and civic sectors.
Winner Notification	Chapter EWISP chairs notify winners in April or May.
Awards	Each participating chapter gives scholarship awards of varying amounts. National corporate awards are between $1,000 and $5,000.
Advice	There are chapters across the United States. Check the website to find the chapter nearest you.

Competition	**The Exploratory Latin Exam**
Sponsor	Excellence Through Classics for Elementary and Middle School Levels
Web Address	http://www.etclassics.org/pages/the-exploratory-latin-exam
Area	Foreign language
Competition Origin	2002
Purpose	To recognize and foster interest in the classical world.
Description	Students answer 30 multiple-choice questions on a variety of topics. Tests are administered through the student's schools and the teacher sends the tests to be judged.
Eligibility	The competition is open to students in grades 3–6. Entry forms and a syllabus including topics for questions are located on the website.
Important Dates	Tests can be administered from October 1 through April 1.
How to Enter	Registration forms must be submitted and are available through a link on the website.
Judging Criteria	The students with the highest scores will be announced as the winners.
Judges	Scorekeepers will tally the scores of each entry.
Winner Notification	Winners will be announced in May.
Awards	All participants will receive ribbons, high scorers will receive certificates, and perfect scorers will earn medallions.
Advice	Check the website for updates to deadlines, rules, and regulations. Sample exams are available to help students prepare for the test.

57

Competition	**Federal Junior Duck Stamp Program**
Sponsor	U.S. Fish and Wildlife Service The Federal Duck Stamp Program 4401 North Fairfax Dr. Mail-Stop: MBSP 4070 Arlington, VA 22203
Web Address	http://www.fws.gov/juniorduck/
Areas	Science and visual arts
Competition Origin	1989
Purpose	To teach wetlands awareness and conservation through the arts to students.
Description	The JDS program is a curriculum-based art education program. One of the activities suggested in the curriculum guide is designing a Junior Duck Stamp—a stamp that is sold by the Wildlife Service every year—and entering that design in the state JDS contest. Information is mailed to schools in October. Teachers may write to the sponsor for a free curriculum guide and a JDS video. Visit the website for more details.
Eligibility	Students in grades K–12.
Important Dates	Contact the state sponsor as dates vary. Alternatively, visit the website and look for your state's deadlines.
How to Enter	Mail your design to your state sponsor.
Judging Criteria	Accurate depiction of wildlife in its natural habitat.
Judges	Each state selects five judges.
Winner Notification	Winners are notified in November.
Awards	Recognition and prizes will vary from state to state; however, all entries will receive certificates of participation and winners will receive special ribbons. In acknowledgment of the integral part teachers and parents play in education and the future of the youth of our nation, the national winner and one parent or guardian will receive a free trip to participate in the First Day of Sale ceremony in late June/early July. Cash prizes of up to $5,000 are also awarded.
Advice	Download the competition rules and entry forms from the website.

Competition	**Fire Fighting Home Robot Contest**
Sponsor	Trinity College Fire Fighting Robot Contest 190 Mohegan Dr. West Hartford, CT 06117
Web Address	http://www.trincoll.edu/events/robot
Area	Technology
Competition Origin	1994
Purpose	To build a computer-controlled robot that can find and extinguish a fire in a house.
Description	Students of all ages build computer-controlled, programmed robots that perform a necessary function in the home. Guidelines may be obtained on the website or by writing to the sponsor.
Eligibility	Anyone of any age or ability. The contest is open to groups or individuals.
Important Dates	The annual competition is held in late spring. See guidelines for specific dates.
How to Enter	Contact the sponsor.
Judging Criteria	The capability of the robot to quickly find and extinguish a fire in a house.
Judges	University-appointed judges.
Winner Notification	Winners are announced at the competition.
Awards	There are cash prizes for the top robots in each division. There are also non-cash prizes given and these vary each year.
Advice	Get the rules and start working early. You can also see pictures of previous winning robots on the website.

Competition	**Freedoms Foundation National Awards Program**
Sponsor	Freedoms Foundation at Valley Forge 1601 Valley Forge Valley Forge, PA 19481
Web Address	http://www.freedomsfoundation.org/National-Awards.cfm
Area	Language arts and social studies
Competition Origin	1949
Purpose	To publicly honor and recognize the exceptional efforts of individuals, organizations, corporations, and schools who promote, through words or deeds, an understanding of responsible citizenship and the benefits of a free society.
Description	Most youth category entries are in the form of written essays and speeches. However, projects for individual achievement or involvement in communities are also welcome. Eligible material must have been written, developed, or released during the awards year. Guidelines are available year-round on the website or by contacting the sponsor.
Eligibility	Students in grades K–12.
Important Dates	Deadline for entries is in June. See guidelines for specific dates.
How to Enter	Submit scrapbook, ring binder, photo album, video or CD-ROM of substantiating material. Include items such as news clippings, photo, letters of commendation, programs, etc. A one-page summary must be included with the entry stating why it should be selected for a Freedoms Foundation National Award.
Judging Criteria	The jury is instructed to review the one-page summary and look favorably on current programs and projects.
Judges	National Awards Jury is comprised of chief and associate State Supreme Court justices and executive officers from National Veteran Service and civic clubs, veterans, or educational organizations.
Winner Notification	Winners are notified in the fall.

Awards

Top recipient in the Youth Category receives a U.S. Savings Bond and framed George Washington Honor Medal. All other recipients receive a George Washington Honor Medal.

Advice

Winning entries from other local/national contests are eligible. Entries may not be the product of classroom assignments.

Competition	**Future City Competition**
Sponsor	National Engineers Week Future City Competition 1420 King St. Alexandria, VA 22314
Web Address	http://www.futurecity.org
Areas	Engineering, mathematics, and science
Competition Origin	1984
Purpose	To promote interests in math, science, and engineering by providing an engineering challenge that is hands-on as students create their city for the future.
Description	Students work as a team with an educator and engineer mentor to plan cities using SimCity™ 4 Deluxe software; research and write solutions to an engineering problem; build tabletop scale models with recycled materials; and present their ideas before judges at Regional Competitions in January. Regional winners represent their region at the National Finals in Washington, DC in February.
Eligibility	Students in grades 6–8.
Important Dates	Competition materials are mailed in mid-August. Regional competitions end in late January. The national competition is held in mid-February. See guidelines for specific dates.
How to Enter	Teams of students must register on the website.
Judging Criteria	Students are judged on computerized design, physical model, essay, and verbal presentation.
Judges	Engineers and teachers appointed by the regional and national coordinators.
Winner Notification	Winners are announced on-site at regional and national levels.
Awards	The first-place winner receives a trip to U.S. Space Camp in Huntsville, Alabama. The first runner-up receives up to $5,000 in scholarships for his or her school's technology program. A second runner-up also receives $2,000 in scholarships for his or her school's technology program.
Advice	Teams need an engineer mentor to assist with projects.

Competition	**Future Problem Solving Program**
Sponsor	Future Problem Solving Program International 2015 Grant Place Melbourne, FL 32901
Web Address	http://www.fpspi.org
Areas	Creativity/problem solving and language arts
Competition Origin	1974
Purpose	To motivate and assist students to develop and use creative thinking skills; learn about complex issues that will shape the future; develop an active interest in the future; develop and use written and verbal communication skills; learn and utilize problem solving strategies; develop and use teamwork skills; develop and use research skills; and develop and use critical and analytical thinking skills.
Description	The regular program consists of teams of four given a futuristic "fuzzy" situation with which they must brainstorm problems, identify an underlying problem, brainstorm solutions to that problem, set criteria for judging the solutions, rank the top solutions, and pick the best solution. The individual program is a scaled down version of the regular program, consisting of just one participant. The scenario writing program has participants write short stories on designated topics taking place in the future. The community problem solving program has a team of any size identify a real life problem, follow the regular program steps to a best solution, and finally implement its solution. Contact the Future Problem Solving Program for guidelines.
Eligibility	Students in grades 4–12. There are three grade divisions: Junior (4–6); Intermediate (7–9); and Senior (10–12).
Important Dates	Each state has its own deadlines for when the problems are due. For the Open Division, the qualifying problem is due by mid-March. The International Conference is held during the second weekend in June. See guidelines for specific dates.
How to Enter	Contact the Future Problem Solving Program or visit the website.

Judging Criteria	Contact the sponsor for information on judging criteria.
Judges	Evaluators for the International Conference are nominated by their state affiliate directors and chosen from a pool of all of those who are nominated.
Winner Notification	Winners are announced at the competition.
Awards	The awards for winning the various competitions vary from state to state. The norm includes trophies and/or plaques. Winners at the International Conference are also awarded trophies and/or plaques.
Advice	To achieve the highest possible scores, participants are advised to utilize the practice problems, research the topic thoroughly, and keep an open mind for all possible solutions to their problem.

Competition	**George S. and Stella M. Knight Essay Contest**
Sponsor	National Society of Sons of the American Revolution 1000 S. 4th St. Louisville, KY 40203-3208
Web Address	http://www.sar.org/node/190
Areas	Language arts and social studies
Competition Origin	1988
Purpose	The contest is designed to give high school students an opportunity to explore events that shaped American history.
Description	The contest is for an original, researched, and proven topic written in English. The topic of the essay should deal with: an event, person, philosophy, or ideal associated with the American Revolution; the Declaration of Independence; or the framing of the United States Constitution. Students must cite at least five references with the minimum of three being printed references. References from encyclopedias or all electronic references will not be accepted as source material and will cause the essay to be disqualified. The essay must have a minimum of 750 words and not exceed 1,000 words excluding title page, footnotes, bibliography, and biography. Contact local affiliates or visit the national website for guidelines.
Eligibility	Students in grades 10–12.
Important Dates	State affiliates should be contacted for local dates.
How to Enter	The contest must be entered through a Chapter of the Sons of the American Revolution near the student's residence.
Judging Criteria	Essays are judged on the following criteria: historical accuracy; clarity of thought; organization and proven topic; grammar and spelling; and documentation.
Judges	Local, state, and national judges are appointed by the SAR.
Winner Notification	Winners are notified by state chapters upon completion of competition, and national winners are notified prior to Annual Congress.

Awards

State and Chapter prizes vary. The National Society awards are: first place, $2,000, a winning recognition plaque, and airfare and hotel for one night at the SAR Annual Congress; second place, $2,000; and third place, $1,000. The winning essay of the national contest will be submitted for publication in *The SAR Magazine*.

Competition	**Get Ready for Winter Photo Contest**
Sponsor	Power to Learn: Optimum Education Initiative and The Weather Channel 1111 Stewart Ave. Bethpage, NY 11714
Web Address	http://www.powertolearn.com/weather_channel_contest/index.shtml
Area	Visual arts
Competition Origin	2013
Purpose	To remind students of the importance of being prepared for winter by depicting preparations at home for a storm, proper attire, winter sports, or even tickets to a tropical vacation.
Description	Entrants submit one original photograph depicting preparations for winter.
Eligibility	Students in a Cablevision serviceable area in grades 3–12. There are two categories, category 1 (grades 3–7) and category 2 (grades 8–12).
Important Dates	The contest is run between December and February each year.
How to Enter	Photos must be submitted online or by e-mail as a .jpg or .jpeg file of high resolution but less than 10MB in size. See website for up-to-date details.
Judging Criteria	Student photos are judged based on conveyance of the theme (25%), composition (25%), creativity (25%), and photographic quality (25%).
Judges	The sponsors' independent selection panel.
Awards	Category 1 prize winners receive a pair of Beats Tour In-Ear Headphone. Category 2 winners receive a GoPro camera. Schools with prize winners receive a wireless professional weather center.
Winner Notification	Winners are notified through their parent or legal guardians' contact details.
Advice	All entries must be submitted with the completed Official Entry Form.

Competition	**Graphic Communications Week Poster Design Contest**
Sponsor	International Graphic Arts Education Association, Inc. (IGAEA)
Web Address	http://www.igaea.org/International-Graphic-Arts-Education-Association/gcw-poster-contest.html
Area	Visual arts
Competition Origin	2004
Purpose	To give students the opportunity to symbolize the power and importance of printed communication through visual art.
Description	Students design a poster for Graphic Communications Week, which typically revolves around Benjamin Franklin's birthday (January 17). The theme can encompass anything that symbolizes the power and importance of printed communications. Visit the website for guidelines.
Eligibility	Students in grades 9–12.
Important Dates	Posters must be received by mid-July. See guidelines for specific dates.
How to Enter	Students can download an application from the website. All entries must be mailed to the coordinator for each year's competition (the name and address are printed on the entry form).
Judging Criteria	Adherence to entry guidelines and a poster that symbolizes the power and importance of printed communications.
Judges	Appointed by the sponsor.
Winner Notification	Winners are notified in time for the annual summer conference.
Awards	$300 for first-place winners, and cash prizes of varying amounts for second- and third-place winners. Winning posters are displayed at the annual summer conference.
Advice	Check website for updates.

Competition	**The Harvard-MIT Mathematics Tournament**
Sponsor	MIT Department of Mathematics Massachusetts Institute of Technology Department of Mathematics Headquarters Office Building 2, Room 236 77 Massachusetts Avenue Cambridge, MA 02139-4307
	Harvard Department of Mathematics Department of Mathematics FAS Harvard University One Oxford Street Cambridge, MA 02138 USA Jane Street Capital; Two Sigma
Web Address	http://web.mit.edu/hmmt/www/
Area	Mathematics
Competition Origin	1998
Purpose	To promote math skills for talented students
Description	Three individual tests (Algebra, Geometry, and Combinatorics) and two team events (the Team Round and the Guts Round) will comprise the major events of the tournament.
Eligibility	Six-member teams of high school students are eligible to enter. Each school may register three teams.
Important Dates	October 15 is the deadline for entry into the competition.
How to Enter	See website for registration forms. There are two competitions: one in February (considered to be the more difficult of the two) and one in November.
Judging Criteria	Teams with the highest overall scores will be named the winners.
Judges	Aaron Landesman and Eric Mannes are the head graders for the tournament.
Winner Notification	Winners will be announced at the competition.
Awards	Prizes will be presented at the completion of the competition to the 10 highest scoring individuals overall, the 10 highest scorers on each of the subject rounds, the five highest scoring teams in the Team

69

Round, and the five highest scoring teams in the Guts Round.

Advice   Check website for deadline changes and complete rules for competing teams.

Competition	**Hispanic Heritage Month Essay Contest**
Sponsor	Power to Learn: Optimum Education Initiative 1111 Stewart Ave. Bethpage, NY 11714
Web Address	http://www.powertolearn.com/hispanic_heritage_month/index.shtml
Area	Language arts
Competition Origin	2008
Purpose	To celebrate Hispanic heritage month by recognizing Latinos who are admired by young people.
Description	Entrants submit an original essay, in 500 words or less, in response to the question "Who is a Latino you admire and why?" The person could be someone from their community, someone who has had an impact on their lives, or any Latino of their choice.
Eligibility	Students in a Cablevision serviceable area in grades 6–12. There are two categories, middle school (grades 6–8) and high school (grades 9–12).
Important Dates	The contest is run between September and December each year.
How to Enter	Essays can be submitted online, by email or postal services. See website for up-to-date details.
Judging Criteria	Student essays are judged based on comprehension, organization, conclusions, creativity and writing.
Judges	The sponsors' independent selection panel.
Awards	Each category has a grand prize of $2,500 cash scholarship; 1st place is a tablet computer; 2nd place is a laptop computer; and 3rd place is a netbook.
Winner Notification	Winners are announced the second week in January on the website.
Advice	All entries must be submitted with the completed Official Entry Form.

Competition	**HOBY Sophomore Leadership Seminars**
Sponsor	Hugh O'Brian Youth Foundation (HOBY) 31255 Cedar Valley Drive, Ste. 327 Westlake Village, CA 91362
Web Address	http://www.hoby.org
Area	Leadership
Competition Origin	1958
Purpose	To seek out, recognize, and develop leadership potential among high school sophomores and to promote understanding among this group of America's Incentive System.
Description	Schools select a student who best represents their community's concept of an outstanding sophomore student leader. Contact the sponsor for guidelines.
Eligibility	Students in grade 10.
Important Dates	Nomination forms are sent to all high schools in the fall. Forms must have been returned by the high schools to the Los Angeles office for guaranteed acceptance by mid-November. The final deadline for acceptance is the end of February. See guidelines for specific dates.
How to Enter	Apply to principal and/or guidance counselor.
Judging Criteria	Prospective students are asked to complete three essay questions on the form: How have you: 1) demonstrated leadership ability? 2) expressed sensitivity and concern for others? 3) shown the desire to learn and share knowledge and experience with others?
Judges	Each student applicant's school principal or guidance counselor is the judge. A school "selection panel" may also be formed.
Awards	Upon selection, the student will be allowed to attend one of HOBY's 91 leadership seminars in his or her state free of charge. At this seminar the student will interact with identified leaders in the fields of business, industry, science, arts, education, and government.

Winner Notification

Notifying the school winner is the responsibility of each school.

Advice

The vast majority of HOBY's work is done through its 4,000 volunteers across the U.S., Canada, Mexico, and the Bahamas. There is no cost to the student, school, or parent. From each local leadership seminar, one boy and girl are selected to attend HOBY's week long World Leadership Congress (WLC) in July at no cost. The WLC is held in a different city each year and is coordinated by a major university.

Competition	**Illustrators of the Future Contest**
Sponsor	L. Ron Hubbard's Illustrators of the Future Contest (Author Services, Inc.) P.O. Box 3190 Los Angeles, CA 90078
Web Address	http://www.writersofthefuture.com/
Area	Visual arts
Competition Origin	1988
Purpose	To encourage and acknowledge aspiring illustrators.
Description	This is a contest for amateur artists. Students should submit three color or black-and-white illustrations. Mixed-media, computer-generated art, and photography are accepted. Each illustration must represent a different subject.
Eligibility	The contest is open only to those who have not professionally published and been paid for more than three black-and-white story illustrations or more than one color-process painting.
Important Dates	Entries are accepted year round. There are four quarters of competition: the first begins on October 1, the next on January 1, the third on April 1, and the last on July 1.
How to Enter	You may only enter once in each quarter of the year. You can send in hard copies or submit electronically. See the website for details.
Judging Criteria	Illustrations must be of a science fiction or fantasy nature. Quarter winners are invited to participate in the Grand Prize Contest, in which they will be asked to illustrate one of that year's winning Writers of the Future stories. The winning illustrations are chosen based on the extent to which they make the judges want to read the story.
Judges	All judges are professional artists. A complete list of current and past judges with short biographies can be found on the website.
Winner Notification	Winners in each quarter will be individually notified of the results by phone, mail, or e-mail.

Awards

Three awards of $500 are made quarterly, with an annual grand prize of $5,000 awarded to one winner. Each winner will also receive a trophy.

Advice

Applicants should check the website to confirm rules and details.

Competition	**Intel International Science and Engineering Fair**
Sponsor	Science Service Inc. 1719 N Street NW Washington, DC 20036
Web Address	http://www.societyforscience.org/isef
Areas	Engineering, science, mathematics, and technology
Competition Origin	1950
Purpose	To promote science and education by providing a formalized structure for more than 400 affiliated science fairs.
Description	Students advance from local, regional, state, and national science fairs to compete at the ISEF. Contact your local science fair coordinator or the sponsor for details.
Eligibility	Students in grades 9–12. Each ISEF affiliated fair may send up to two finalists and one team project to the ISEF.
Important Dates	Contact sponsor for dates of local, regional, and state fairs. The national fair is held in May each year.
How to Enter	Complete application and forms as distributed by the sponsor.
Judging Criteria	Vary with each level of competition.
Judges	At the national level, judges are international experts from the fields of science, mathematics, and engineering.
Winner Notification	Winners are announced at the conclusion of each fair.
Awards	$50,000 in scholarships are given to the top three winners. There is also the opportunity to advance to contests in other countries, and there are several cash awards.
Advice	Talk to your school's science fair coordinator to get started.

Competition	**Intel Science Talent Search**
Sponsor	Science Service 1719 N Street NW Washington, DC 20036
Web Address	http://www.societyforscience.org/sts
Areas	Engineering, mathematics, and science
Competition Origin	1942
Purpose	To foster the education of young potential scientists, mathematicians, and engineers.
Description	Entering high school seniors submit a written report of an independent science, mathematics, or engineering research project. Guidelines are available in mid-August or through the website.
Eligibility	Students entering grade 12.
Important Dates	Entry materials are available for request in mid-August. Entries must be received by mid-November. See guidelines for specific dates.
How to Enter	Contact sponsor for official rules and entry form, or obtain an entry form on their website.
Judging Criteria	Evidence of creativity and interest in science.
Judges	A team of more than 20 judges specializing in a variety of scientific disciplines.
Winner Notification	In late January, the finalists are notified. The top scholarship winners are notified in March.
Awards	Three hundred semi-finalists benefit in the following ways: (1) recommendations to colleges and universities for admission and financial assistance; (2) certificates of achievement for students and teachers; and (3) a fine sense of accomplishment and a measure of self–esteem that come from finishing a hard assignment. The 40 finalists, selected from the semi-finalists, are also awarded a trip to Washington, DC, for the 5-day all-expenses-paid Science Talent Institute for final judging and a chance to share $205,000 in scholarships.
Advice	The research project must be the work of a single individual. Group projects are not eligible.

Competition	**International Aviation Art Contest**
Sponsor	National Aeronautic Association (NAA), in association with the National Association of State Aviation Officials (NASAO) and sponsored by Embry-Riddle Aeronautic University—Prescott, Ken Cook Co., the Federal Aviation Administration, and the National Coalition for Aviation and Space Education
Web Address	http://www.nasao.org/TEST/Center/InternationalAviationArtContest.aspx
Area	Visual arts
Competition Origin	1989
Purpose	To illustrate the importance of aviation through art.
Description	An art competition using watercolor, acrylic, oil paint, indelible marker pens, felt-tip pens, soft ball point pens, indelible ink, Crayola crayons, or any similar indelible medium depicting an aviation theme as designated by the current year's competition.
Eligibility	Students between the ages of 6 and 17. Complete competition rules are available on the website.
Important Dates	Entries are submitted in January.
How to Enter	Art work should be submitted on 11 3/4" x 16 1/2" medium without a frame or outline. Registration forms are available through a link on the website.
Judging Criteria	Three categories based on age and creative use of the theme in relation to the aviation world.
Judges	Judges will be knowledgeable in art and aviation.
Winner Notification	Winners will be notified at the completion of each segment.
Awards	The top three state winners will have their entries forwarded to the national competition. National winners receive certificates, ribbons, and a framed reproduction of their artwork, and the original is sent to the international competition. Winners of the international competition receive certificates and gold, silver, or bronze medals.
Advice	Consult website for current theme, registration forms, and changes in deadlines. Information for state competitions and contact information is also available on the website.

Competition	**International Brain Bee**
Sponsor	Society for Neuroscience
Web Address	http://www.internationalbrainbee.com
Area	Science
Competition Origin	1998
Purpose	To test the neuroscience knowledge of students and to inspire them to pursue careers in the biomedical brain research field.
Description	Students compete in a question-and-answer competition. Guidelines can be obtained through the website.
Eligibility	Students in grades 9–12.
Important Dates	The International Brain Bee is held in mid-March. Local and regional dates may vary. See guidelines for specific dates.
How to Enter	Contact your local coordinator or visit the website for details.
Judging Criteria	Accuracy of answers.
Judges	Neuroscientists organize and judge the competition.
Winner Notification	Winners are announced on-site.
Awards	IBB prizes include scholarships, travel awards, trophies, and research assignments. Currently, the winner of the International Brain Bee Championship will be awarded $3,000, a summer research fellowship with an acclaimed neuroscientist, and a traveling trophy for display at his or her school. The second-place finisher will receive $2,000 and the third-place finisher will receive $1,000.
Advice	The sponsor's website includes links to some excellent study resources.

Competition	**International Schools CyberFair**
Sponsor	Global SchoolNet. Foundation 270 N. El Camino Real, Ste. 395 Encinitas, CA 92024
Web Address	http://www.globalschoolnet.org/gsncf/index.cfm
Areas	Social studies and technology
Competition Origin	1996
Purpose	For students, their schools, and their local communities to use the Internet to share resources, establish partnerships, and work together to accomplish common goals.
Description	Students research one of eight categories in their local communities and publish their findings to the Internet. The schools with the best project in each of the eight categories are recognized. Visit the website for competition details, suggestions, and former projects.
Eligibility	Students ages 5–19.
Important Dates	Register between October and March. See guidelines for specific dates.
How to Enter	Register online. This is a collaborative project, and each team must consist of students and teachers.
Judging Criteria	The peer review rubric evaluates theme, content, organization, conventions, appearance, and technical elements. Rubrics can be viewed on the website.
Judges	There is a peer review process for this competition. Additionally, candidates for an international Review Board of distinguished Internet and education professionals are selected based on their experience and devotion to online collaborative learning and their reputation as visionaries of the Global Information Infrastructure.
Winner Notification	Winners are notified in May.
Awards	Each school or organization that completes a final entry receives a special CyberFair certificate to proudly display in its community. Top projects receive a 1-year subscription to *Futurist* magazine. Projects that best

Advice

illustrate "future thinking" are invited to the World Future Society international conference.

Check the website for categories and updated submission dates.

Competition	**International Student Media Festival**
Sponsor	ISMF c/o AECT P.O. Box 2447 Bloomington, IN 47402-2447
Web Address	http://www.ismf.net/
Areas	Technology and visual arts
Competition Origin	1980
Purpose	To encourage student media production.
Description	Students enter a media production in one of the following areas: live action, animation, sequential stills, interactive stills, website, photographic essay, and single photograph. Judges are obligated to watch only the first 7 minutes of the entry, but entries can be as long as deemed fit. Guidelines may be obtained on the website or by writing to the sponsor.
Eligibility	Students in grade K–12 and college. There are four grade divisions: K–4, 5–8, 9–12, and college.
Important Dates	Entries are accepted from March through May. See guidelines for specific dates.
How to Enter	Sign up and join the organization's mailing list.
Judging Criteria	Creativity/originality, organization/purpose, continuity/structure, relevance/importance, use of available resources, clarity, energy/education, residue, technical quality, and general effectiveness.
Judges	The judges consist of educators knowledgeable in technology.
Winner Notification	Winners are notified in November.
Awards	Students receive certificates and critiques. Winners can also attend an awards ceremony. There are also some special awards with details on the website.
Advice	There are fees that must be submitted with each entry.

Competition	**Jane Austen Society of North America Essay Contest**
Sponsor	Jane Austen Society of North America
Web Address	http://www.jasna.org/essaycontest/index.html
Area	Language arts
Competition Origin	1979
Purpose	To foster the study and appreciation of Jane Austen.
Description	The essay has a topic each year and the target audience is for those that are interested in the life and work of Jane Austen. References should not exceed five sources. Submissions must be made by e-mail.
Eligibility	High school, college students, and post-graduate students.
Important Dates	May 15 is the deadline for entries.
How to Enter	Entries must be submitted with an official Essay Contest entry form that is available through a link on the website as a Word document.
Judging Criteria	Essays will be judged on original insights and clear, correct writing.
Judges	Persons knowledgeable in English and Literature will rank the essays entered.
Winner Notification	Winners will be posted on jasna.org in September.
Awards	First-place winners receive a $1,000 scholarship, second-place winners receive a $500 scholarship, and third-place winners receive a $250 scholarship. Winners also receive a Jane Austen book and registration with two nights' lodging for the JASNA's Annual General Meeting in Minneapolis, Minnesota.
Advice	Check the website for changes in deadlines and contest rules.

Competition	**Japan Bowl**
Sponsor	The Japan-American Society of Washington 1819 L Street, NW, 1B Level Washington, DC 20036
Web Address	http://www.us-japan.org/dc/japanbowl.php
Area	Foreign language
Competition Origin	1992
Purpose	To recognize excellence in Japanese language and culture.
Description	The Japan Bowl is modeled on a quiz show format and aims to make the study of Japanese challenging and enjoyable. Teams of students are asked questions regarding Japanese culture, grammar, kanji, katakana, kotowaza, and onomatopoeic expressions. The winners of the Regional Japan Bowl Competitions are eligible to compete at the National Japan Bowl Competition in Washington, DC. The guidelines can be downloaded from the website.
Eligibility	Students in grades 9–12 who are currently enrolled in Levels II, III, and IV Japanese language classes.
Important Dates	The national bowl is held in Washington, DC, in the spring of each year. Regional dates vary, so you should check the website for the one nearest your school.
How to Enter	To participate in the Japan Bowl, students must complete and submit the application and agreement forms to their regional Japan Bowl host organization by the specified deadline, which is to be determined by the regional host.
Judging Criteria	Performance in team and toss-up questions.
Judges	Appointed by sponsor.
Winner Notification	Winners are recognized on the day of the bowl, but must be present at the awards ceremony to receive their prizes.
Awards	Certificates and plaques are given to winning teams. The first-place national winners receive a trip to Japan. Regional awards vary, but those winning at the regional level go on to the national bowl.
Advice	Sample questions are available on the website in the entry requirements and information guide.

Competition	**John F. Kennedy Profiles in Courage Essay Contest**
Sponsor	John F. Kennedy Library Foundation Profiles in Courage Essay Contest Columbia Point Boston, MA 02125
Web Address	http://www.jfkcontest.org
Areas	Language arts and social studies
Competition Origin	1994
Purpose	To encourage high school students to write a compelling essay on the meaning of political courage and to learn about and be inspired by America's elected officials, past or present, who have tried to make a difference in the world.
Description	In fewer than 1,000 words, students write an essay that is original, creative, and demonstrates an understanding of political courage as described by John F. Kennedy in *Profiles in Courage*. Students are to use a variety of sources such as newspaper articles, books, and/or personal interviews to write about one of the given topics.
Eligibility	Students in grades 9–12.
Important Dates	Entries can be submitted between September and January. See guidelines for specific dates.
How to Enter	Applications can be downloaded from the website. Essays can be submitted online or by mail. Contestants must have a teacher sponsor for guidance and support.
Judging Criteria	Essays are judged on content (55%) and presentation (45%).
Judges	A national panel of judges selected by the Kennedy Library.
Winner Notification	Winners are notified in April.
Awards	The winner receives $10,000 and is invited to the Kennedy Library in May to accept his or her award. A second-place winner receives $1,000. Five finalists each receive $500. All winners receive a hardcover copy of John F. Kennedy's *Profiles in Courage*. The nominating teacher of the first-place winner is invited

Advice

to the Kennedy Library in May to receive the John F. Kennedy Public Service Grant in the amount of $500 for school projects encouraging student leadership and civic engagement. All participants receive a certificate of participation.

See the website for more specific essay topic information.

Competition	**Joseph S. Rumbaugh Oration Contest**
Sponsor	National Society Sons of the American Revolution 1000 S. Fourth St. Louisville, KY 40203
Web Address	http://www.sar.org/node/38
Areas	Language arts and social studies
Competition Origin	1945
Purpose	To bring American history to the high school student and focus on events of today; to draw an intelligent relationship between the past and the present; to clearly demonstrate freedom of opportunity as a basic right of our national heritage; to place a positive emphasis on the plans of our founding fathers; to emphasize justice under law in a free society; and to illustrate how the Revolutionary War influenced our freedom of expression.
Description	The contest is for an original oration of 5–6 minutes. Topics shall deal with an event, personality, or document within the context of the Revolutionary War and the relationship it bears to America today. Contact your state society or the national office for guidelines. Rules are also available online.
Eligibility	Students in grades 9–12.
Important Dates	Dates vary with level of competition. The national entries must be submitted 2 weeks prior to the annual conference. See guidelines for specific dates.
How to Enter	Participate at the local, state, and district levels.
Judging Criteria	Judging will be based on composition, delivery, significance and history.
Judges	Members of the Sons of the American Revolution.
Winner Notification	National winners are recognized at the annual Congress on the National Society of the Sons of the American Revolution.
Awards	National winners receive scholarship awards.
Advice	Contact state sponsor early in the school year.

Competition	**Junior Science and Humanities Symposium**
Sponsor	U.S. Army, Navy, and Air Force
Web Address	http://www.jshs.org/about.html
Area	Science, engineering, and math.
Competition Origin	1958
Purpose	To promote original research and experimentation in the sciences, engineering, and mathematics at the high school level.
Description	Competitors will conduct original research in one of seven categories listed on the website: http://www.jshs.org/forms/Ntl%20student%20guidelines.pdf. A written abstract of 200 words is required and an oral presentation is to be made upon request of the judges. Research papers that are 5–20 pages long should be submitted detailing research performed and results of the research.
Eligibility	High school students
Important Dates	Forms and reports are due by April 3.
How to Enter	Research papers must be prepared and oral presentations must be delivered according to the National JSHS Program Fact Sheet and Guidelines for Students that is available on the website.
Judging Criteria	Judging is based on six areas with a possible 30 points for each area. See complete judging criteria on the website.
Judges	The National JSHS Judging Team includes individuals who hold either a Ph.D. or equivalent experience or who are actively engaged in research.
Winner Notification	Winners are announced at the various regional and national symposia.
Awards	Seven $12,000 undergraduate tuition scholarships are awarded to the first place finalists in the national research paper competition; seven $8,000 undergraduate tuition scholarships are awarded to the second place finalists and seven $4,000 undergraduate tuition scholarships are awarded to the third place finalists.

Advice

View complete rules and regulations on the website.
Tips for presentations are also offered. Check for
changes in deadlines.

Competition	**Kids Are Authors**
Sponsor	Kids Are Authors Scholastic Book Fairs 1080 Greenwood Blvd. Lake Mary, FL 32746
Web Address	http://www.scholastic.com/bookfairs/contest/kaa_about.asp
Areas	Language arts and visual arts
Competition Origin	1986
Purpose	To encourage students to interact and cooperate as a team, while at the same time using their reading, writing, and artistic skills.
Description	Kids Are Authors is a picture book writing and illustration competition. Each entry must be the result of a cooperative effort of three or more students. The winning entry is published in a hardcover edition by Scholastic Books. Guidelines may be obtained on the website.
Eligibility	Students in grades K–8.
Important Dates	Deadline for entries is mid-March. See guidelines for specific dates.
How to Enter	Groups of three or more students can enter this competition by writing and illustrating their own previously unpublished, original picture book. Each entry must be accompanied by a completed official entry form (available from the website).
Judging Criteria	Entries are judged on originality, story content, illustrative quality, and compatibility of text and illustrations.
Judges	Judges are selected by Scholastic Book Fairs from professionals in the fields of children's literature, art, and education.
Winner Notification	Winners are notified by the end of May.
Awards	Two winning schools (one for fiction, one for nonfiction) receive $5,000 in merchandise, framed certificates, medallions, and 100 copies of their published book. Twenty-five honor awards may be

selected; honor winners receive $500 in merchandise for their schools and certificates.

Advice

Start with a group brainstorming session on story ideas. Once the group has come to a consensus on the story line, the children should begin asking themselves what is the best way to express that concept through words and illustrations. Introduce children to various art techniques and allow them to experiment with the one that works best for them. Bold images in bright colors often work best. Project coordinators and students may want to read and review previous Kids Are Authors winners for inspiration. Check website for updates to rules and regulations.

Competition	**Kids Philosophy Slam**
Sponsor	Kids Philosophy Slam P.O. Box 406 Lanesboro, MN 55949
Web Address	http://www.philosophyslam.org
Areas	Philosophy and visual arts
Competition Origin	2000
Purpose	To give students a voice and encourage them to think using their creative potential through philosophical forums.
Description	Students use a theme presented by the contest and submit an original piece of work such as a painting, essay, song, or other artwork. Guidelines may be obtained on the website or by writing to the sponsor.
Eligibility	Students in grades K–12.
Important Dates	Entries should be postmarked by early February. See guidelines for specific dates.
How to Enter	Mail your entry to the sponsor.
Judging Criteria	Creativity, originality, and overall strength of the message the student is conveying. For some competitions, the strength of one's argument is also judged.
Judges	A panel of philosophers, educators, and parents.
Winner Notification	Finalists are notified in late March.
Awards	There are more than $3,000 in prizes, including certificates, T-shirts, and U.S. savings bonds awarded.
Advice	Visit the website for resources and ideas.

Competition	**Knowledge Master Open (KMO)**
Sponsor	Academic Hallmarks, Inc. P.O. Box 998 Durango, CO 81301
Web Address	http://www.greatauk.com/KMO.html
Area	Academic quiz bowl
Competition Origin	1983
Purpose	To provide opportunities for all motivated students to participate in a national and international academic competition without the attendant expenses of traveling to a central site, and to give students from schools, large or small, urban or rural, a chance to objectively compare their achievement with thousands of the best students in the country's top schools.
Description	Teams in the Knowledge Master Open receive curriculum-based contest questions (200 at secondary levels; 100 at 5th and 6th grade levels) on a CD-ROM and compete using a computer at their own schools. The event is held twice each year. Up to 4,000 schools and 60,000 students from the U.S. and several foreign countries participate in KMO. Rules from previous competitions are available for the asking or by visiting the website. Also, rules and suggestions are sent along with the contest kits. The kits are mailed so that materials arrive at the schools about 10 days in advance of the contest date.
Eligibility	Students in grades 5–12.
Important Dates	The elementary KMOs are held in January and March annually. The secondary KMOs take place in December and April. See guidelines for specific dates.
How to Enter	Entry forms are available on the website.
Judging Criteria	Accuracy of answers. Winners are those teams in each of the national, state, and enrollment divisions who accumulate the greatest number of points.
Judges	Self-scoring.
Winner Notification	Winners are notified the day after the competition.
Awards	Division winners receive plaques and shirts. All teams receive a poster, stickers for the individual

team members, and certificates of participation. All participating schools receive a complete set of results showing the rankings of all teams in the various divisions. A substantial number of top teams are written up in their local newspapers, some have received congratulatory letters from the president, and others have appeared on CNN and NBC.

Advice

For teams and coaches who have not participated before, it is generally a good idea to become familiar with the format of the event by working with a practice disk. The practice disks are simply the contest disks from previous years. At the end of each KMO, participants are given a special password that turns the contest disk into a practice disk. Teams will benefit by learning to communicate clearly and effectively in the context of the event and to apply various strategies for maximizing their scores.

Competition	**Laws of Life Essay Competition**
Sponsor	John Templeton Foundation 300 Conshohocken State Road, Ste. 500 West Conshohocken, PA 19428
Web Address	http://www.acelebrationofspirit.org/laws-of-life/
Area	Language arts
Competition Origin	1987
Purpose	To encourage students to discover values that will help them through life.
Description	Students are encouraged to write on any topic relating to experiences and people that have shaped their values and lives. Guidelines may be obtained through the website.
Eligibility	Students in grades K–12 and college.
Important Dates	Local contest dates vary. Check the website for contest locations and deadlines.
How to Enter	Contact the sponsor in order to receive an information kit. There is some information on their website.
Judging Criteria	Students are judged based on compelling content, presentation, and grammar and spelling.
Judges	Local community members.
Winner Notification	Winners are announced at the awards ceremony.
Awards	An awards banquet is held for the contest finalists and their families. Certificates and other awards are presented at the banquet. Local prizes may vary depending on sponsorship.
Advice	This contest is held locally, but it is a worldwide event.

Competition	**Letters About Literature Competition**
Sponsor	The Library of Congress 101 Independence Ave, SE Washington, DC 20540
Web Address	http://www.read.gov/contests/
Area	Language arts
Competition Origin	1999
Purpose	To allow students an opportunity to express their personal feelings about a book.
Description	Students write a letter to an author of their choice explaining how the author's work has changed their way of thinking about the world and themselves. Contact the sponsor for a teacher's guide or download guidelines from the website.
Eligibility	Students in grades 4–12. There are three grade divisions: Level I (4–6); Level II (7–8); and Level III (9–12).
Important Dates	Letters are due in early December. See guidelines for specific dates.
How to Enter	Select a book you read recently about which you have strong feelings. You need not like the characters or even the way the events in the book turn out in order to be affected by the story. Write a letter of 750 words or less(check your category for number of words) to the author, explaining what the book taught you about yourself. Make a connection between yourself and a character or an event in the book.
Judging Criteria	Exposition, content, and writer's voice are the criteria used for judging.
Judges	Library of Congress appointees.
Winner Notification	Winners are notified in April.
Awards	State winners advance to the national competition and receive cash prizes. One national winner per level of competition receives $1,000 cash award and one second place winner receives $150 cash.
Advice	The letter should let the author know how the book made you feel, what impact the book had on you, etc. It is not recommended that you summarize the book.

In other words, think of the audience to whom you are writing—the person who will read the letter. Be honest, personal, and conversational, as if the author were a friend who would write back to you.

Competition	LifeSmarts Championship
Sponsor	Western Union National Consumers League Attention: LifeSmarts 1701 K St. NW, Ste. 1200 Washington, DC 20006
Web Address	http://www.lifesmarts.org/
Area	Business
Competition Origin	2000
Purpose	To teach consumer literacy.
Description	LifeSmarts is an interactive education program that teaches students the skills they need to be consumer savvy in today's marketplace. With the support of a coach, players work together to form teams and compete in online, regional, and national competitions.
Eligibility	Students in grades 6–12.
Important Dates	State online competition dates are listed on the website.
How to Enter	Register online for the state competition; winners will go on to compete in the national competition.
Judging Criteria	Highest scorers of the timed test will be declared the winning team.
Judges	Judges are from national and international corporations that are knowledgeable in consumer literacy.
Winner Notification	The winning team will be notified at the national competition.
Awards	Members of the winning team will each receive one $1,000 scholarship and one $1,000 U.S. savings bond.
Advice	See the website for complete rules and topics.

Competition	**The Lions International Peace Poster Contest**
Sponsor	Lions Clubs International 300 W. 22nd St. Oak Brook, IL 60523-8842
Web Address	http://www.lionsclubs.org/EN/our-work/youth-programs/peace-poster-contest/index.php
Area	Visual arts
Competition Origin	1988
Purpose	To give young people the opportunity to express their thoughts about world peace in an original artwork.
Description	Posters are judged at the school level and there are two more rounds to reach international competition and the grand prize. Themes change from year to year; for example, the theme for 2012 was "Our World, Our Future." Teachers and principals must contact Lions Clubs International for guidelines. There is also information on the website.
Eligibility	Students ages 11–13 (on November 15).
Important Dates	Fall deadlines for submitting posters vary according to district, and national deadlines are in early December. See guidelines for specific dates.
How to Enter	School teachers or principals should contact Lions Clubs International or obtain an application form online. Lions Clubs must purchase a competition kit (available in mid-January).
Judging Criteria	Posters are judged according to originality, artistic merit, and expression of theme.
Judges	Throughout the judging process, posters are evaluated by different groups of judges. On the international level, they are judged by internationally renowned people involved with art, peace, or children.
Winner Notification	Winners are announced at each level of competition. International winners are notified at the beginning of February.
Awards	One international grand prize winner will receive $5,000 and a trip to a special award ceremony with the sponsoring club president and two family members at Lions Day with the United Nations

(subject to change). Each of the 23 merit-award winners will receive a cash award of $500 and a certificate of achievement. Winning artwork is published on the website. Local recognition varies.

Advice

No one may enter the contest independently. Students and schools must be sponsored by a local Lions Club to participate.

Competition	**The Louise Louis/Emily F. Bourne Student Award of the Poetry Society of America**
Sponsor	Poetry Society of America Annual Award Submission 15 Gramercy Park New York, NY 10003
Web Address	http://www.poetrysociety.org/psa/awards/annual/individual/
Area	Language arts
Competition Origin	2000
Purpose	To promote the writing of poetry.
Description	This competition is for unpublished poetry from high school students.
Eligibility	High school students
Important Dates	Submissions must be postmarked between October 1 and December 22.
How to Enter	Students may send a single entry for $5, or teachers or administrators may send an unlimited amount of their students' work (one submission per student) for a fee of $20. A cover sheet is required for each submission. For details, see the guidelines on the website.
Judging Criteria	Good writing skills and originality.
Judges	Current year judges are listed on the website.
Winner Notification	Winners will be posted on the Poetry Society of America's website.
Awards	Students are granted a $250.00 award for submitting a winning poem.
Advice	Check the website for changes in deadlines and complete entry regulations. There is a cover sheet template available on the website.

Competition	**Mandelbrot Competition**
Sponsor	Greater Testing Concepts The Mandelbrot Group P.O. Box 760 Potsdam, NY 13676
Web Address	http://www.mandelbrot.org
Area	Mathematics
Competition Origin	1990
Purpose	To introduce high school students to all levels of mathematics while providing stimulating and challenging problems.
Description	This is a 40-minute math competition that allows for group and individual work. Guidelines can be found on the website.
Eligibility	Students in grades 9–12.
Important Dates	Contests are administered from October until March. See guidelines for specific dates.
How to Enter	You may enter this contest by registering on the website.
Judging Criteria	Accuracy of answers.
Judges	Graded by teachers and coaches.
Winner Notification	Results are announced within a month of each round of competition.
Awards	Individual and team awards vary, but include Mandelbrot playing cards.

Competition	**Manningham Student Poetry Awards**
Sponsor	National Federation of State Poetry Societies 7059 Spring Valley Road Dallas, TX 75254
Web Address	http://www.nfsps.com/student_awards.htm
Area	Language arts
Competition Origin	1959
Purpose	To encourage and support the writing of poetry.
Description	Students can submit poems of any form on any subject and up to 50 lines. A contest brochure can be sent if a self-addressed, stamped envelope is mailed to the sponsor. Guidelines are also available online.
Eligibility	Students in grades 6–12. There are two grade divisions: Junior (6–8) and Senior (9–12).
Important Dates	The deadline for entry is in March. See guidelines for specific dates.
How to Enter	Send a poem (limit one per student) to the coordinator for submission.
Judging Criteria	Must be an original poem.
Judges	Judged anonymously by a poet who is a member of NFSPS with expertise in judging and chosen from prizewinners in other annual contests.
Winner Notification	Winners are notified in early May.
Awards	First prize wins $75, second prize wins $50, third prize wins $40, fourth prize wins $35, and five honorable mentions win $10 each. Winning poems are published in an anthology.
Advice	Using correct grammar and an interesting title will get attention for your poem. Check the website for any updates.

Competition	**The Marie Walsh Sharpe Art Foundation Summer Seminar**
Sponsor	The Marie Walsh Sharpe Art Foundation 725 N. Tejon St. Colorado Springs, CO 80903
Web Address	http://sharpeartfdn.qwestoffice.net/summer1.htm
Area	Visual arts
Competition Origin	1987
Purpose	To offer an intensive visual art studio program for high school juniors.
Description	Students submit an application form with 6–10 copies of at least four individual works, two of which must be drawings; a written statement expressing the most memorable experience of his or her life; and a recommendation from a high school art teacher. All details are located on the website or can be obtained by writing to the sponsor after January. Brochures are mailed to all public and private schools in January.
Eligibility	Students in grade 11.
Important Dates	Application deadline is in April. See guidelines for specific dates.
How to Enter	Contact the sponsor or download the application from the website.
Judging Criteria	Judges will assess quality and originality in the primary rounds with recommendations and written statements being reviewed in the final round.
Judges	A panel of jurors designated by the foundation select the participants for the summer seminar.
Winner Notification	Winners are notified in late May.
Awards	Full-tuition awards including tuition, room, board, and all seminar-related expenses are provided. Transportation is not included.
Advice	Students need a recommendation from an art teacher, summarizing (a) their creative potential for original work, (b) how they interact with others, and (c) any other factors including aspects of character, personality, and health that bear on the applicant's ability to participate in the summer seminar program.

Competition	**MATHCOUNTS**
Sponsor	MATHCOUNTS Foundation 1420 King St. Alexandria, VA 22314
Web Address	http://mathcounts.org
Area	Mathematics
Competition Origin	1983
Purpose	To promote student math achievement.
Description	MATHCOUNTS is a national math coaching and competition program that promotes math achievement through grassroots involvement in every U.S. state and territory. Guidelines may be obtained on the website or by writing to the sponsor.
Eligibility	Students in grades 6–8.
Important Dates	Kits are distributed to schools in September. The registration deadline is in December. See guidelines for specific dates.
How to Enter	The school completes and forwards the application to the sponsor.
Judging Criteria	Vary with math-related area of competition.
Judges	Professionals in mathematics and related areas.
Winner Notification	Winners are announced at each level of competition.
Awards	Individual and team awards at regional and national levels vary.

Competition	**Mathematical Olympiads for Elementary and Middle Schools**
Sponsor	Mathematical Olympiads for Elementary and Middle Schools 2154 Bellmore Ave. Bellmore, NY 11710-5645
Web Address	http://www.moems.org
Area	Mathematics
Competition Origin	1979
Purpose	To encourage students to appreciate and cultivate a love for mathematics.
Description	Five contests (Olympiads) are administered during the school year, given from November to March. Guidelines may be obtained online.
Eligibility	Students in grades 4–8.
Important Dates	Enrollments are due by the end of September. See guidelines for specific dates.
How to Enter	Write for registration form and other information, or have your school enroll online.
Judging Criteria	Each Olympiad contains five open-ended questions with a time limit on each. If a student gets a correct answer, he or she receives a point and his or her team is credited with one point.
Judges	Scorekeepers tally the scores at the end of each round. The team with the highest points wins.
Awards	Each participant receives a certificate of participation. The high scorer of each team receives a trophy. Other awards include Olympiad patches, pins, medallions, and plaques.
Winner Notification	Winners are notified in April.
Advice	There are costs associated with this competition, so talk to your mathematics teacher to get started. The website also contains sample problems and lots of important information.

Competition	**Medusa Mythology Exam**
Sponsor	Medusa Mythology Examination P.O. Box 1032 Gainesville, VA 20156
Web Address	http://www.medusaexam.org
Area	Classical literature/mythology
Competition Origin	1995
Purpose	The Medusa was developed in order to allow those talented in mythology an opportunity to excel and be recognized. Another aim is to increase students' exposure to mythology.
Description	The Medusa is composed of 50 multiple-choice questions, and the exam has a different theme every year. In the fall, a flyer, registration form, and syllabus will automatically be mailed to those schools where students have participated in the past. If you would like to have your school added to the mailing list, please contact the Medusa Exam Committee. You may also download the registration materials from the website.
Eligibility	Students in grades 6–12 (or age 11 or higher if homeschooled).
Important Dates	The exam is administered in early April each year. See guidelines for specific dates.
How to Enter	Register online or via mail.
Judging Criteria	Accuracy of answers.
Judges	The Medusa Exam Committee, a team of 10 professors, teachers, and students, design the syllabus and questions for the exam. In addition, a panel of esteemed teachers reviews the initial copy of the exam to ensure its complete mythological accuracy. The Medusa Exam Committee then reviews the final copy of the exam.
Winner Notification	Winners are notified in May.
Awards	Top achievers on the exam receive certificates or medals imported from Italy. The highest-scoring participants can apply for several achievement awards to assist with educational expenses. Special awards are

107

given for middle-school students and teachers whose students take the exam.

Advice

Past exams can be downloaded from the website. There is a small fee for participation. Be sure to check the website for updates in rules and regulations as well as for exam administration dates.

Competition	**Modern Woodmen of America School Speech Contest**
Sponsor	Modern Woodmen of America Attn: Fraternal Department Youth Division 1701 1st Ave., P.O. Box 2005 Rock Island, IL 61204-2005
Web Address	http://www.modern-woodmen.org/MemberBenefits/ YouthPrograms/YouthEducationalPrograms/Pages/ SchoolSpeechContest.aspx
Area	Language arts
Competition Origin	1948
Purpose	To learn public speaking skills as well as how to reinforce English skills and build self-esteem.
Description	Each school year there is a new topic. Students get 3–5 minutes to discuss that topic. Topics usually come from suggestions by teachers who use the program. Guidelines and applications are available on the website or by contacting your local Modern Woodmen representative.
Eligibility	Students in grades 5–12, but with a focus on grades 5–8. At the national level, the competition is only for students in grades 5–8.
Important Dates	Arranged by local schools. Contests can be held anytime from January through May.
How to Enter	Contact your local Modern Woodmen representative to arrange for a speech contest in your school.
Judging Criteria	Speeches are judged on material organization, delivery, presentation, and overall effectiveness.
Judges	Appointed by local school for first level of competition and by the sponsor for regional and national levels.
Winner Notification	Winners of competitions are recognized on-site.
Awards	The winners of each school's Speech Contest can advance to the higher levels. At the national level, contestants compete for savings plans. The savings plans, plus interest, will be paid to the winners when they become of legal age.
Advice	The contest may not be available in all parts of the country.

Competition	**M³ (Moody's Mega Math) Challenge**
Sponsor	The Moody's Foundation and the Society for Industrial and Applied Mathematics (SIAM)
Web Address	http://m3challenge.siam.org/
Area	Mathematics
Competition Origin	2006
Purpose	To promote problem solving using mathematics.
Description	Three- to five-member teams made up of high school juniors and seniors compete to solve the current year's Challenge Problem mathematically. The Challenge Problem can be found on the webpage.
Eligibility	High schools located in the following states are eligible to participate in the M³ Challenge: Alabama, Connecticut, Delaware, Florida, Georgia, Illinois, Indiana, Kentucky, Louisiana, Maine, Maryland, Massachusetts, Michigan, Minnesota, Mississippi, New Hampshire, New Jersey, New York, North Carolina, Ohio, Pennsylvania, Rhode Island, South Carolina, Tennessee, Vermont, Virginia, Washington D.C., West Virginia, and Wisconsin.
Important Dates	Registration deadline is February 22.
How to Enter	Enter online through the website. Teams must have a teacher-coach to enter.
Judging Criteria	Judges will select the most successful solution to the current year's Challenge Problem.
Judges	A panel of professional applied mathematicians
Winner Notification	Winners will be announced following the competition.
Awards	A $20,000 scholarship to be shared by the winning team.
Advice	Check for updates to regulations and deadlines.

Competition	**NASA Space Settlement Contest**
Sponsor	NASA Ames Research Center and the National Space Society Al Globus/Mail Stop 262-4 Bldg. 262, Rm. 277 Moffett Field, CA 94035-0001
Web Address	http://settlement.arc.nasa.gov/Contest/
Area	Science, technology, engineering, mathematics, visual arts, and language arts
Competition Origin	1994
Purpose	To promote the study and development of space settlements.
Description	This is a multifaceted competition featuring designs, original research, essays, stories, models, artwork or any other orbital space settlement related materials.
Eligibility	Group and individual entries for students in grade 7 and under, 8, 9, 10, 11, and 12. Groups can consist of two to six members.
Important Dates	Entries must be received by March 15.
How to Enter	Complete rules can be found on the website, where you can also obtain entry forms.
Judging Criteria	Original, creative work that focuses on space settlements that are self-sufficient.
Judges	NASA Ames Contractor Council
Winner Notification	Winners will be presented at the national conference.
Awards	The highest scoring individual or group project will receive $5,000. All entrants will receive a certificate.
Advice	Check the website to determine location and date of national conference and any changes in rules or deadlines.

Competition	**National Americanism Poster Contest**
Sponsor	National Society, Sons of the American Revolution 1000 S. 4th St. Louisville, KY 40203-3208
Web Address	http://www.sar.org/Youth/ Americanism_Poster_Contest
Area	Visual arts
Competition Origin	2000s
Purpose	To promote Americanism among youth.
Description	All students must address the theme, which changes annually. Any media of drawing material may be used. Entries must be on standard size poster board (22" x 28"). Contact the sponsor for guidelines.
Eligibility	Students in grades 3–5.
Important Dates	Local and state deadlines vary. The national deadline is in July. See guidelines for specific dates.
How to Enter	Contact your state chapter.
Judging Criteria	Posters are judged on expression of theme, originality, evidence of research, artistic merit and creativity, accuracy of reflection of historical events, neatness, and visual appeal.
Judges	Local and national judges.
Winner Notification	Varies with local contest dates.
Awards	The winners for each state are displayed during the national contest. During the Youth Awards Luncheon, held annually at the National Congress, winners of first, second, and third place will be awarded a Rosette Ribbon and a monetary prize.
Advice	Contact your local or state chapter early in the school year for details.

Competition	**National Current Events League**
Sponsor	National Current Events League Box 2196 St. James, NY 11780-0605
Web Address	http://www.continentalmathematicsleague.com/ncel.html
Area	Social studies
Competition Origin	1993
Purpose	To improve knowledge of current events.
Description	Meets are held 4 times a year at your local school, and each meet consists of 30 multiple-choice questions. Guidelines may be obtained on the website or by writing to the sponsor.
Eligibility	Students in grades 4–12.
Important Dates	Schools need to register by mid-October. See guidelines for specific dates.
How to Enter	Register by mail to the sponsor. The application can be downloaded from the website.
Judging Criteria	Accuracy of answers.
Judges	Each test is proctored and scored by the school using the scoring sheet provided.
Winner Notification	Winners are notified in April.
Awards	Medals and certificates are given to winners.
Advice	Costs are involved for each team registration, so talk to your teacher or principal.

Competition	**National Economics Challenge**
Sponsor	The Council for Economic Education and State Farm
Web Address	http://www.councilforeconed.org/events/national-economics-challenge/
Area	Business
Competition Origin	1953
Purpose	To foster interest in economics among high school students.
Description	Students compete in rounds of testing, work to solve case problems, and participate in an oral quiz-bowl based on economics and current events.
Eligibility	The competition is open to students in grades 9–12.
Important Dates	Teams must be registered by April 9.
How to Enter	Teams of three or four must be entered by their coach. See website for complete rules.
Judging Criteria	The teams with the highest scores will be announced as the winners.
Judges	Scorekeepers will tally the scores of each team.
Winner Notification	Winners will be announced at the national competition.
Awards	National winners will be awarded $1,000 for first place, $500 for second place, $250 for third place, and $250 for fourth place.
Advice	Check the website for updates to deadlines, rules, and regulations.

Competition	National Federation of Music Clubs Competitions
Sponsor	National Federation of Music Clubs 1646 W. Smith Valley Rd. Greenwood, IN 46142
Web Address	http://www.nfmc-music.org
Area	Performing arts
Competition Origin	1898
Purpose	To develop and enhance student skills in music.
Description	Scholarships and awards in music are granted through a variety of student competitions. More information and the guidelines are available on the website.
Eligibility	Each competition has different age categories and guidelines, with competitions open to students in their junior and senior years of high school, as well as to university students and adults. Students should check eligibility requirements for each scholarship or award.
Important Dates	Varies with the competitions. See guidelines for specific dates.
How to Enter	Write to sponsor for scholarship and awards chart or browse the website.
Judging Criteria	Exemplifies excellence in area of competition.
Judges	Music professionals.
Winner Notification	Varies with the competitions.
Awards	More than $750,000 competition and award prizes are awarded on the local, state, and national level.

Competition	**National Federation of Press Women High School Communications Contest**
Sponsor	National Federation of Press Women P.O. Box 5556 Arlington, VA 22205
Web Address	http://www.nfpw.org/highSchoolContest.cfm
Area	Journalism
Competition Origin	1998
Purpose	To recognize excellent journalistic work, inspiring young journalists to perform to the best of their abilities for themselves and their teachers.
Description	In the contest, students may enter work in one of 20 categories: Editorial, Opinion, News Story, Feature Story, Sports Story, Columns, Feature Photo, Sports Photo, Cartooning, Review, Graphics/ Photo Illustration, Single-Page Layout, Double-Truck Layout, Environment, Video News Story, Video Feature Story, Video Sports Story, Yearbook Layout, Yearbook Photo, and Yearbook Copywriting. Guidelines may be obtained on the website or by writing to the sponsor.
Eligibility	Students in grades 9–12.
Important Dates	Each state determines its deadline to allow time for judging and processing for the national contest, so inquire early in the school year. The work must have been completed during the current year. See guidelines for specific dates.
How to Enter	Contact state affiliate or visit the website.
Judging Criteria	See the contest guidelines for specific judging criteria for each contest.
Judges	National Federation of Press Women officials at state and national levels.
Winner Notification	Winners are announced at an awards luncheon held at each year's national conference.
Awards	Certificates are given to all winners at the High School Communications Contest Awards Luncheon, with a first-place cash prize of $100. Assistance from

state affiliates might be available to support student travel to the event.

Advice

Those residing in a state with no National Federation of Press Women affiliate may compete nationally on an at-large basis.

Competition	**National Garden Clubs High School Distinguished Service Project**
Sponsor	National Garden Clubs, Inc. 4401 Magnolia Avenue St. Louis, MO 63110
Web Address	http://www.gardenclub.org/youth/contests/high-school-distinguished-service-project.aspx
Area	Service learning
Competition Origin	1961
Purpose	To encourage civic responsibility.
Description	Projects beneficial to the environment by way of landscape design, conservation, horticulture, or similar domains are developed by students for their communities. Students submit photos and descriptions to a state Garden Club competition, and winners move on to regional and national competitions.
Eligibility	Students in grades 9–12.
Important Dates	See the website for deadline entries for state, regional, and national competitions.
How to Enter	Contact your local garden club for nomination information or visit the website for the email contact for the chairman of this award.
Judging Criteria	Projects will be judged on greatest civic impact and creativity.
Judges	Judges chosen display knowledge of art, horticulture, and/or the environment.
Winner Notification	Winners will be announced at the National Garden Clubs, Inc. Annual Meeting.
Awards	The first-place winner receives $100 and the second-place winner receives $50.
Advice	Check the website for changes in rules and deadlines.

Competition	**National Garden Clubs High School Essay Contest**
Sponsor	National Garden Clubs, Inc. 4401 Magnolia Avenue St. Louis, MO 63110
Web Address	http://www.gardenclub.org/youth/contests/high-school-essay-contest.aspx
Area	Language arts
Competition Origin	1961
Purpose	To promote the conservation and preservation of natural resources.
Description	Students enter original essays about the current year's theme. (Topics are listed on the website.)
Eligibility	Students in grades 9–12.
Important Dates	Deadlines for local, regional, and national entries are on the website.
How to Enter	Enter a 600–700 word essay through a local or state Garden Club, who must sponsor the contest.
Judging Criteria	Essays will be judged on content, composition, and manuscript.
Judges	Judges familiar with art, English composition, and conservation are recruited for the competition.
Winner Notification	The National Winner will be announced at the National Garden Clubs, Inc. Annual Meeting.
Awards	The National Winner receives a $1,000 scholarship.
Advice	Check the website for updates in rules and deadlines as well as for links to complete rules and local Garden Clubs.

Competition	**National Garden Clubs Poetry Contest**
Sponsor	National Garden Clubs 4401 Magnolia Avenue St. Louis, MO 63110
Web Address	http://www.gardenclub.org/youth/contests/high-school-essay-contest.aspx
Area	Language arts
Competition Origin	1961
Purpose	To promote awareness of horticulture.
Description	Students enter original poetry about the current year's theme. (Topics are listed on the website.) Poems may be traditional verse, acrostics, blank verse, cinquains, diamond poems, limericks, or haiku.
Eligibility	Students in grades K–9.
Important Dates	Deadlines for local, regional, and national entries are linked on the website.
How to Enter	Poems must be entered through a local chapter of a Garden Club; winning poems will be forwarded to regional and national competitions.
Judging Criteria	Essays will be judged on title, content, creativity, and style.
Judges	Persons knowledgeable in literature will judge this contest.
Winner Notification	Winners are announced at the National Garden Clubs, Inc. Annual Meeting.
Awards	Winning entries are compiled into a booklet.
Advice	Check the website for updates in rules and deadlines as well as for links to complete rules and local Garden Clubs.

Competition	**National Garden Clubs Youth Sculpture Contest**
Sponsor	National Garden Clubs, Inc. 4401 Magnolia Avenue St. Louis, MO 63110
Web Address	http://www.gardenclub.org/youth/contests/youth-sculpture-contest.aspx
Area	Visual arts
Competition Origin	1961
Purpose	To create structures from recyclable materials as one way to ensure a greener planet.
Description	Create an original sculpture using recycled materials submitted to a state Garden Club competition; winners will be forwarded to regional and national competitions.
Eligibility	Students in grades 4–8.
Important Dates	See the website for deadline entries for state, regional, and national competitions.
How to Enter	Entry form is available on the website and should include as many photos of the sculpture as will fit on the back of the entry form.
Judging Criteria	Entries are judged based on creative use of materials and self-expression, description of sculpture and materials used, and craftsmanship and technique.
Judges	Judges will have a background in recycling and/or art.
Winner Notification	Winners are announced at the National Garden Clubs, Inc. Annual Meeting
Awards	The national winner receives a $1000 scholarship.
Advice	Check the website for current themes, as well as changes in rules and deadlines.

Competition	**National Geographic Bee**
Sponsor	National Geographic Society 1145 17th St. NW Washington, DC 20036-4688
Web Address	http://www.nationalgeographic.com/geobee/
Area	Social studies
Competition Origin	1989
Purpose	To encourage the teaching and study of geography.
Description	Principals of schools must register and each school conducts the first competition, consisting of both oral and written elements. The school winners are then given a qualifying test, and top scorers move on to state competitions; top performers at this stage can move on to the national level. Write to the National Geographic Society for details or visit the website.
Eligibility	Students in grades 4–8.
Important Dates	School competitions are held in mid-November through mid-January. State competitions are held in early spring. National competitions are held in late May. See guidelines for specific dates.
How to Enter	Principals must register their schools before the October deadline to participate in the program. The application form is available online.
Judging Criteria	Based on correctness and completeness of answers to oral and written questions concerning geography.
Judges	At the school and qualifying test levels, a school representative is the judge. A state bee coordinator administrates at the state level, and the National Geographic Society administrates the national competition.
Winner Notification	Winners are announced on the date of competition.
Awards	The national first-place winner receives a $25,000 college scholarship, second place receives a $15,000 college scholarship, and third place receives a $10,000 college scholarship.
Advice	There are some helpful study materials available on the website. The school must pay a fee to receive the contest materials, and at least six eligible students must compete.

Competition	**National High School Oratorical Competition**
Sponsor	The American Legion National Headquarters P.O. Box 1055 Indianapolis, IN 46206-1055
Web Address	http://www.legion.org/oratorical
Areas	Language arts and social studies
Competition Origin	1938
Purpose	To develop a deeper knowledge and appreciation of the U.S. Constitution. Other objectives include leadership, the ability to think and speak clearly and intelligently, and preparation for the acceptance of the duties and responsibilities, as well as the rights and privileges, of American citizenship.
Description	Prepared orations must be based upon the Constitution of the United States. Assigned topics, which follow the prepared orations, are also based on the Constitution. All contestants speak on the same assigned topics. Prepared orations must be 8–10 minutes in length, with the assigned topics running from 3–5 minutes. Guidelines may be obtained on the website or by writing to the sponsor.
Eligibility	Students in grades 9–12.
Important Dates	Department (state) contests are usually held during the month of March. Dates for the National Regionals and Sectionals and the National Finals Contest are determined by The American Legion National Americanism Commission and are published in the annual Oratorical Contest Rules brochure. These contests are usually held during the month of April.
How to Enter	Contact your local, state, or National American Legion Headquarters (The Americanism and Children and Youth Division).
Judging Criteria	Contact the sponsor for information on judging criteria.
Judges	Each contest uses five judges. Judges are typically from the legal profession, educators, the media, and the clergy.
Winner Notification	Winners are announced at each level of competition.

Awards

A National Scholarship fund of more than $100,000 is provided by The American Legion Life Insurance Committee and divided among regional and national winners. National first-place winners receive $18,000, second-place winners receive $16,000, and third-place winners receive $14,000.

Advice

The National Organization of The American Legion will pay the travel cost of department winners and their chaperones as they progress in the national competition. All contestants must be accompanied by a chaperone.

Competition	**National History Day Contest**
Sponsor	National History Day, Inc. 4511 Knox Road, Ste. 102 College Park, MD 20740
Web Address	http://nationalhistoryday.org/Contest.htm
Area	Social studies
Competition Origin	1974
Purpose	To encourage the study of social studies by guiding students to express themselves creatively through presentations of historical topics in various formats.
Description	National History Day is a yearlong educational program that fosters academic achievement and intellectual growth in secondary school students. By participating in a series of district, state, and national competitions, students develop research and reading skills, refine presentation and performance skills, and develop critical thinking and problem-solving skills that will help them manage and use information effectively now and in the future. Guidelines are available on the website.
Eligibility	Students in grades 6–12. There are two grade divisions: Junior Division (6–8) and Senior Division (9–12).
Important Dates	Check the website or contact your state sponsor in late summer or early fall for details.
How to Enter	Contact your state sponsor.
Judging Criteria	Varies with area of competition.
Judges	Professionals such as educators and historians.
Winner Notification	Winners are announced at the contest.
Awards	At each level of competition, outstanding achievement may be recognized through certificates, medals, trophies, monetary awards, scholarships, or special prizes that may vary from year to year.
Advice	Successful History Day entries include not only a description of the topic, but analysis and interpretation. It is important to place your topic into historical context and perspective. Ask yourself the following questions about your topic: Why is my

topic important? How was my topic significant in history in relation to the History Day theme? How did my topic develop over time? How did my topic influence history? How did the events and atmosphere (social, economic, political, and cultural aspects) of my topic's time period influence my topic in history?

Competition	**The National Latin Exam**
Sponsor	National Latin Exam University of Mary Washington 1301 College Ave. Fredericksburg, VA 22401
Web Address	http://www.nle.org
Area	Foreign language
Competition Origin	1978
Purpose	To promote an in-depth understanding of Latin.
Description	Each exam is 40 minutes long and consists of 40 multiple-choice questions. Each exam tests students in the understanding of Latin grammar, comprehension, mythology, life, history, derivatives, and passages. Guidelines are listed on the website.
Eligibility	Students enrolled in Latin or who have completed a course during the academic school year.
Important Dates	The Latin exams are given during the second full week in March. The exam must be mailed by mid-March. See guidelines for specific dates.
How to Enter	An application form can downloaded through the National Latin Exam website. A registration fee of $4 (U.S.) or $6 (outside the U.S.) is also required of students.
Judging Criteria	The exams are graded for grammar, comprehension, content, and historical accuracy.
Judges	Exams are scored by software.
Winner Notification	Results are mailed out in April of each year.
Awards	Certificates, medals, ribbons, and $1,000 scholarships are given.
Advice	The website has a set of helpful FAQs (Frequently Asked Questions).

Competition	**National Leadership Award and "I Dare You!" Scholarship**
Sponsor	American Youth Foundation 6357 Clayton Road St Louis, MO 63117
Web Address	http://www.ayf.com/books/nla#
Area	Leadership
Competition Origin	1941
Purpose	To recognize the leadership capacity of high school students and 4-H participants.
Description	Students are nominated for the National Leadership Award. Recipients of the awards are eligible for an "I Dare You!" Scholarship, which provides funds toward tuition for the American Youth Foundation Leadership Conference. The program is intended to focus on "emerging" leaders—those young adults who have the qualities and abilities to lead, but who may not yet recognize or have acted on their leadership potential. An application form is available on the website or can be requested in writing from the sponsor.
Eligibility	Students ages 15–18.
Important Dates	Contact the sponsor for details.
How to Enter	Complete the selection form provided by sponsor.
Judging Criteria	Recognition by peers and adults who work with students serving as emerging leaders.
Judges	American Youth Foundation officials.
Winner Notification	Winners are notified by the beginning of June.
Awards	The National Leadership Award consists of three elements: a personalized award certificate, a copy of *I Dare You!*, and eligibility to apply for a scholarship to the International Leadership Conferences.
Advice	Scholarships are awarded on a first-come, first-serve basis.

Competition	**National Mythology Exam**
Sponsor	Excellence Through Classics American Classical League Miami University 422 Wells Mill Drive Oxford, OH 45056
Web Address	http://www.etclassics.org/pages/ the-national-mythology-exam
Area	Classical literature/mythology
Competition Origin	1989
Purpose	To acquaint students with mythology and classical literature, including African and Native American myths.
Description	Students take a multiple-choice exam on mythology and classical literature. Guidelines may be obtained on the website or by writing to the sponsor.
Eligibility	Students in grades 3–9.
Important Dates	Registration is by mid-January. Administration of exam is usually in late February or early March. See guidelines for specific dates.
How to Enter	Contact sponsor in writing or enter online.
Judging Criteria	Accuracy of answers.
Judges	Exams are scored by machines.
Winner Notification	Winners are notified in late April.
Awards	Prizes include certificates of excellence and bronze medallions.
Advice	The website has sample questions and study guidelines available online.

Competition	**National Peace Essay Contest**
Sponsor	United States Institute of Peace 2301 Constitution Ave, NW Washington, DC 20037
Web Address	http://www.usip.org/npec
Areas	Language arts and social studies
Competition Origin	1996
Purpose	To promote serious discussion among high school students, teachers, and national leaders about international peace and conflict resolution; complement existing curricula; and strengthen students' research, writing, and reasoning skills.
Description	Students write an essay on the chosen theme, which may focus on topics such as international affairs, conflict resolution, social studies, history, or politics. The competition guidelines and application forms are available on the website.
Eligibility	Students in grades 9–12.
Important Dates	The deadline for entry is early February. See guidelines for specific dates.
How to Enter	Students submit a 1,500-word essay on the chosen topic. Three copies are sent to the sponsor with an application form.
Judging Criteria	Each aspect of the given topic must be addressed. Entries are judged for their research, analysis, and form.
Judges	Essays are sent to state-level judges who are appointed by the Institute.
Winner Notification	Winners are notified in May.
Awards	First-place state winners receive college scholarships of $1,000. First-place state winners also compete for national awards of $10,000, $5,000, and $2,500 (for first, second, and third place, respectively; national awards include state award amounts). All first-place state winners are invited to attend an all-expenses-paid awards program in Washington, DC, in June.

Competition	**National Portuguese Exam**
Sponsor	American Association of Teachers of Spanish and Portuguese (AATSP)
Web Address	www.aatsp.org
Area	Foreign language
Competition Origin	2003
Purpose	To test student language skills in Portuguese.
Description	Students taking the exams are grouped into levels, depending on their in-class and out-of-class experience with Portuguese. Highest scorers at each level are recognized at the chapter (state) level and national level. Tests are administered at the school setting. Any Portuguese teacher who is an AATSP member in good standing may enter students in the competition. Guidelines may be obtained on the website or by writing to the sponsor.
Eligibility	High school students of Portuguese. The teacher must be a member of AATSP.
Important Dates	Testing takes place between mid-February and mid-March. See guidelines for specific dates.
How to Enter	Teachers need to register their classes by contacting the AATSP.
Judging Criteria	Accuracy of answers.
Judges	Exams are teacher-scored.
Winner Notification	Winners are notified upon completion and scoring of examination.
Awards	Recognition will vary within each school. Students who participate are ranked on the local and national levels based on results.

Competition	**National Rifle Association Youth Wildlife Art Contest**
Sponsor	George Montgomery Foundation and the National Rifle Association
Web Address	http://www.nrahuntersrights.org/Article.aspx?id=6956
Area	Visual arts
Competition Origin	1987
Purpose	To support the Second Amendment of the U.S. Constitution.
Description	This competition is for any artwork of North American wildlife that is legal to hunt or trap. It may not contain images of endangered species or non-game animals or birds.
Eligibility	Students in grades 1–12 are divided into four age categories.
Important Dates	November 5 is the deadline to enter.
How to Enter	Submit an entry form (can be found on the website) and an original artwork. See website for complete rules and information.
Judging Criteria	Entries will be judged on creativity, anatomical accuracy, and effort.
Judges	Judges have knowledge in art as well as animal anatomy.
Winner Notification	Winners are published on the website.
Awards	First place winners in each age category receive cash prizes of $750. $500 and $250 cash prizes are given to second and third-place winners, respectively, and a grand prize of $1000 is given for the Best of Show.
Advice	Check the website for updates to deadlines and rules.

Competition	**National Science Bowl**
Sponsor	U. S. Department of Energy SC-27/ Forrestal Building 1000 Independence Ave., SW Washington, DC 20585
Web Address	http://science.energy.gov/wdts/nsb
Area	Science
Competition Origin	1991
Purpose	To encourage high school students to pursue careers in science and math.
Description	Teams of high school or junior high/middle school students compete in a fast-paced quiz bowl to solve technical problems and answer questions in all branches of science and math.
Eligibility	High school and junior high/middle school students
Important Dates	Teams must register by March 12.
How to Enter	Teams must be entered by their coach/teacher. Complete rules can be viewed on the competition website.
Judging Criteria	Teams with the overall highest scores will be the winners.
Judges	Scorekeepers keep a tally of all rounds to determine the winning team.
Winner Notification	Winners are announced at the National Science Bowl competition.
Awards	The National Science Bowl is held annually at the National 4-H Center, just outside Washington, D.C. Regional teams are invited to compete and given an all-expenses-paid trip to the competition. The top 16 high school teams in the competition's double elimination rounds will each receive $1,000 for their school's science department and a National Science Bowl plaque. The top eight junior high/middle school teams in the double elimination rounds will each receive $1,000 for their school's science department and a National Science Bowl plaque.
Advice	Check the website for changes in prizes, deadlines, and regulations.

133

Competition	**National Social Studies League**
Sponsor	National Social Studies League P.O. Box 2196 St. James, NY 11780-0605
Web Address	http://www.continentalmathematicsleague.com/nssl.html
Area	Social studies
Competition Origin	1993
Purpose	To improve social studies skills.
Description	A multiple-choice test on social studies is administered to participating students. These questions are based on topics in American studies, geography of the United States, and United States government, appropriate to each grade level. Guidelines may be obtained on the website or by writing to the sponsor.
Eligibility	Students in grades 2–12.
Important Dates	The deadline for registration is mid-October. See guidelines for specific dates.
How to Enter	Register by mailing an application to the sponsor. The application can be downloaded from the website.
Judging Criteria	Accuracy of answers.
Judges	Local school officials use sponsor's scoring key. Sponsor tabulates national results.
Winner Notification	Winners are notified in May.
Awards	Medals and certificates to local winners. National winners are also recognized with individual and team awards.
Advice	There are registration fees required for each school's team, so talk to your teacher or principal.

Competition	**National Spanish Examinations**
Sponsors	National Spanish Examinations 2701 Beech Street, Ste. P Valparaiso, IN 46383
Web Address	http://www.nationalspanishexam.org/
Area	Foreign language
Competition Origin	1957
Purpose	To motivate students to learn more about the Spanish language and culture.
Description	Students in grades 6–12 can compete in this online test measuring their abilities and skills in Spanish language learning.
Eligibility	Students in grades 6–12 who are enrolled in a Spanish class.
Important Dates	Exams are given between March and April. See guidelines for specific dates.
How to Enter	Teachers must enter the students. This may be done through the website or by contacting the sponsor.
Judging Criteria	Accuracy of answers.
Judges	Exams are scored by computer.
Winner Notification	Names of national winners are published in the September issue of the American Association of Teachers of Spanish and Portuguese (AATSP) journal.
Awards	Certificates are awarded for high-scoring students. The students with the top five scores at the national level are awarded medals, and there are some scholarships available.
Advice	There are various study materials available on the website.

Competition	**National Young Astronomer Award**
Sponsor	The Astronomical League National Office Manager 9201 Ward Parkway, Ste.100 Kansas City, MO 64114
Web Address	http://www.astroleague.org/al/awards/nyaa/noya.html
Area	Science
Competition Origin	1993
Purpose	To recognize outstanding achievement in astronomy by amateur astronomers.
Description	A national panel of judges selects the winner based upon the student's overall achievements in astronomy. Activities that the judges consider include astronomical research, published astronomical articles, local astronomical club activities, academic achievements in science and math, involvement in regional and national astronomy organizations, observing history and skills, astrophotography and/or CCD imaging, public education experience, and telescope design. Guidelines may be obtained on the website or by writing to the sponsor.
Eligibility	Students in grades 9–12 or who are 14 to 19 years of age and not enrolled in college on the application deadline.
Important Dates	The deadline for submission is late January. See guidelines for specific dates.
How to Enter	Complete the application form and obtain a sponsor's signature. Submit your entry packet in electronic format (Adobe Acrobat PDF files) to NYAA@astroleague.org. Submit a photo of yourself, preferably in an astronomical setting, in jpg format to NYAA@astroleague.org.
Judging Criteria	Award selections are, by their very nature, subjective. Accordingly, the league warrants only that awards will be presented to individuals who, in the opinion of the national judges, merit the awards. Because of staffing constraints and difficulties inherent in the award process, the award chairperson may extend deadlines or respond to special needs and circumstances in administering the award. Judges' rankings are

averaged using Zipf's Law (e.g., a third-place vote equals one-third of a point, a fourth-place vote equals one-fourth of a point). Ties are broken by the lowest total of raw rankings.

Judges

The NYAA committee selects a national panel of judges consisting of well-known amateur and professional astronomers who review all application packages and select 10 finalists. Currently, all judges are professional physicists and astronomers.

Winner Notification

Winners are notified in mid-March.

Awards

The first-place winner receives a Meade 10-inch LX-200 Schmidt-Cassegrain Telescope valued at about $3,000. The winner also receives an all-expenses-paid trip to the League's national convention to receive the award. The University of Texas' McDonald Observatory presents "lifetime passes" to the first- and second-place winners. Plaques are presented to the first-, second-, and third-place winners at the League's national convention each summer.

Advice

Your work should be original research and your sources should be well-documented in a generally accepted format.

Competition	*NewsCurrents* **Student Editorial Cartoon Contest**
Sponsor	NewsCurrents Cartoon Contest P.O. Box 52 Madison, WI 53701
Web Address	http://www.newscurrents.com/intro/edcartoons/carcon2.html
Areas	Journalism and visual arts
Competition Origin	1989
Purpose	To showcase the complex thinking and communications skills young people are capable of when challenged with effective curricular materials.
Description	Entrants must submit original cartoons on any subject of national or international interest. Each entry must include the following information written on the back of the cartoon: student's name, grade, school, school address, school phone number, and the signature of a teacher verifying that the cartoon is the original work of the student. Guidelines are available on the website.
Eligibility	Students in grades K–12. There are three grade divisions: K–6, 7–9, and 10–12.
Important Dates	Entries must be postmarked at a date in March of each year. See guidelines for specific dates.
How to Enter	Mail entries to the sponsor's address.
Judging Criteria	Entries are judged primarily on the basis of originality, clarity of idea, and knowledge of subject. Artistic quality is considered secondarily.
Judges	The judges consist of the editorial staff of *NewsCurrents*.
Winner Notification	Winners will be notified by mid-April.
Awards	First-, second-, and third-place winners are chosen from each grade category. Winners receive U.S. savings bonds. The top two winners are published in an issue of the weekly *NewsCurrents Current Events* program, viewed by more than one million students.
Advice	Judges recommend that cartoons be drawn with black ink on white paper. Use bold lines and make letters large enough to be read easily. Draw the cartoons in a horizontal format. Don't create a cartoon that is

nothing more than a simple slogan or a poster. Be thought provoking and original. Entries sent after the deadline will automatically be entered in the next year's contest.

Competition	**NMA Leadership Speech Contest**
Sponsor	National Management Association 2210 Arbor Blvd. Dayton, OH 45439
Web Address	http://www.nma1.org/Speech_Contest/Speech_Contest.html
Area	Leadership, business, and language arts
Competition Origin	1988
Purpose	To build leadership skills in students.
Description	This is a four-level competition starting at the chapter level, progressing to the council level, then to the regional level, and culminating with the national finals in September or October. Students research, write, and deliver a speech on leadership.
Eligibility	Students in grades 9–12.
Important Dates	Chapter-level competitions begin in January.
How to Enter	Visit the website for complete rules and forms needed to enter this competition.
Judging Criteria	Judging is based on three areas: content (50%), delivery (30%), and language (20%).
Judges	Toastmasters International members
Winner Notification	Winners are announced at each competition.
Awards	The chapter level awards up to $300 for first place, the council level awards up to $500 for first place, the regional level awards the first-place winner $1,000 and the second-place winner $500, and the national level awards $4,000 first place, $1,000 for second place, and two $500 third-place prizes.
Advice	Parents should contact the sponsors of each of the different levels to determine schedules as students must compete in all levels to be eligible for the national level.

Competition	**Odd Fellows & Rebekahs United Nations Pilgrimage for Youth**
Sponsor	I. O. O. F. United Nations Educational Pilgrimage for Youth, Inc. The Independent Order of Odd Fellows 422 Trade Street Winston-Salem, North Carolina 27101-2830
Web Address	http://www.unpilgrimage.org/
Area	Social studies
Competition Origin	1949
Purpose	To study and learn about the United Nations.
Description	Students submit an essay and may be required to participate in a speech contest. Contact your local Odd Fellows and/or Rebekah Lodge for more information.
Eligibility	Students ages 16–17 with at least one year of high school remaining.
Important Dates	The trip takes place during the summer. Application submission dates vary, but Jurisdictional Chairmen must begin submitting deposit fees and delegate information to the Executive Director in January, so make sure to begin the process well in advance. Contact your local Odd Fellows and/or Rebekah Lodge for an application.
How to Enter	Contact your local Odd Fellows and/or Rebekah Lodge. Students must apply through a local sponsoring group and comply with their requirements.
Judging Criteria	Applications are reviewed by committees for evidence of scholarship, leadership, character, extracurricular activities, concern for community welfare, interest in world affairs, and general fitness to participate in the program.
Judges	Members of the Independent Order of Odd Fellows and Rebekahs.
Winner Notification	Winners are notified prior to summer.
Awards	Winners tour the United Nations building and listen to behind-the-scenes briefings conducted by

141

specialized United Nations agencies and departments, as well as visit other sights in New York City. Expenses including transportation, meals, lodging, and sightseeing are paid for by the Odd Fellows and Rebekah Lodges in your community, county, district, state, or province and by donations from corporations and individuals. The student provides spending money for souvenirs, laundry, shopping, extra refreshments, and entertainment.

Competition	**Odyssey of the Mind Program**
Sponsor	Odyssey of the Mind Program c/o Creative Competitions, Inc. 406 Ganttown Road Sewell, NJ 08080
Web Address	http://www.odysseyofthemind.com
Area	Creativity/problem solving
Competition Origin	1978
Purpose	To foster creative thinking and provide creative problem-solving opportunities for all students.
Description	Each team performs its solution within a specified time frame and within certain cost limits. Odyssey of the Mind (OM) charters affiliates that run the local and state (association finals) competitions. These competitions culminate with an International OM World Finals competition held annually in late May or early June. Competing teams in this event represent top finishers in each U. S. state and many international counties. Guidelines may be obtained on the website or by writing to the sponsor.
Eligibility	Students in grades K–12 and college. There are four grade divisions: Division I (K–5); Division II (6–8); Division III (9–12); and Division IV (Collegiate).
Important Dates	Local competitions begin in January and end with the OM World Finals in late May or early June. The OM membership year runs concurrent with the school year. See guidelines for specific dates.
How to Enter	Each member is entitled to participate in the local competition. Registration varies from state to state. Contact your local association director.
Judging Criteria	There is no right or wrong answer to any problem, but there are both limitations and a specific end result that must be achieved. Teams are judged in three areas. The first is in the "long-term" problem: that is, the solution that the team has created and showcases in the competition. The second is style, or how one "markets" or elaborates the solution. This may be achieved by the use of such elements as music, dance, costumes, script, and so on. Finally, spontaneity is judged as a third category. Each team receives

143

a problem to solve the day of the competition. The team must solve it on the spot without any preparation and within a time limit.

Judges

Judges are adult volunteers trained before the competition. Some are educators, some are business people, and others are interested parents, supporters, and former team members.

Winner Notification

Winners are announced at an awards ceremony following each competition.

Awards

Awards vary, but are generally medals, trophies, and certificates.

Advice

Purchase membership materials at the beginning of the school year. Local competitions begin as early as January, and students need time to develop, troubleshoot, and fine-tune solutions.

Competition	**Olympiada of Spoken Russian**
Sponsor	American Councils of Teachers of Russian (ACTR) 1828 L St., NW, Ste. 1200 Washington, DC 20036
Web Address	http://www.americancouncils.org/program/1q/OSR/
Area	Foreign language
Competition Origin	1962
Purpose	This competition is for U.S. high school students to demonstrate excellence in Russian language.
Description	This contest involves speaking about yourself, reading, and the civilization of Russia. Guidelines may be obtained on the website or by writing to the sponsor.
Eligibility	Students in grades 9–12 who are winners of state and regional Olympiada contests.
Important Dates	State competitions must be finalized by late April for participation at the national level. See guidelines for specific dates.
How to Enter	A teacher who is a member of ACTR must enter a student. This can be done through the website or by contacting the sponsor.
Judging Criteria	Spoken fluency of Russian language.
Judges	Teachers of Russian and members of ACTR.
Winner Notification	State winners are notified for participation in national program.
Awards	Medals and certificates are distributed at an awards ceremony held at the school for the winners. The top students in each region (gold medalists) are invited to take part in a summer immersion program in Russia sponsored by ACTR. In addition, every third year, an international Olympiada contest is convened in Moscow, during which students of Russian from around the world and winners of the Olympiadas in their respective countries gather in Moscow to compete for the international medals, as well as engage in a rich program of cultural activities, performances, and juries.
Advice	Entry costs $6 for students. All students must be registered by members of ACTR for the current year. Some states or regions require a school registration fee. American Councils funds all other program costs.

145

Competition	**Patriot's Pen**
Sponsor	Veterans of Foreign Wars of the United States (VFW) & Ladies Auxiliary VFW Building 406 W. 34th St. Kansas City, MO 06411
Web Address	http://www.vfw.org/Community/Patriot-s-Pen/
Areas	Language arts and social studies
Competition Origin	1995
Purpose	To give students the opportunity to express their views on democracy.
Description	Patriot's Pen is a nationwide competition that gives students the opportunity to write essays expressing their views on democracy. Contestants write a 300–400 word essay on a patriotic theme. Students advance from the state competition to the national competition. Visit the website for contest guidelines and contact information for the national headquarters or your local VFW Post.
Eligibility	Students in grades 6–8.
Important Dates	Entries are due at the beginning of November. See guidelines for specific dates.
How to Enter	Contact the national headquarters or your local VFW Post. An entry form and rules can also be downloaded from the website.
Judging Criteria	Knowledge of theme, theme development, and clarity of ideas.
Judges	Appointed by the VFW.
Winner Notification	Winners are notified in March.
Awards	The top 46 national winners all receive at least $500. The first-place award is currently $5,000, plus an all-expense paid trip to Washington, DC for the winner and a parent or guardian.
Advice	Be sure to establish a contact with someone in your local VFW Post or Ladies Auxiliary.

Competition	**Physics Bowl**
Sponsor	American Association of Physics Teachers (AAPT) One Physics Ellipse College Park, MD 20740-3845
Web Address	http://www.aapt.org/programs/contests/physicsbowl.cfm
Area	Science
Competition Origin	1994
Purpose	To encourage interest in physics and recognize students' scientific achievements and excellence in teaching.
Description	All students who enter take a 40-question, timed, multiple-choice test supervised at their school. Contest questions are based on topics and concepts in typical high school physics courses. Guidelines may be obtained on the website or by writing to the sponsor.
Eligibility	Students in grades 9–12. There are two divisions: Division I (first year physics students) and Division II (second year physics students).
Important Dates	Registration is in late March, with the testing during mid-April. See guidelines for specific dates.
How to Enter	Request application materials online or via mail.
Judging Criteria	Accuracy of answers.
Judges	Tests are scored by machines.
Winner Notification	Winners are notified as soon as individual and team scores are submitted and calculated by AAPT.
Awards	All students and teachers who enter the Physics Bowl receive a certificate of participation from the AAPT. T-shirts are awarded to the four top students in the top-scoring school in each region. Other prizes vary each year.

Competition	**Pier 1 Imports®/UNICEF Greeting Card Contest**
Sponsor	UNICEF and Pier 1 Imports United States Committee for UNICEF 333 E. 38th St. New York, NY 10016
Web Address	http://www.unicefusa.org/campaigns/ pier-1-greeting-card-contest/
Area	Visual arts
Competition Origin	1991
Purpose	To allow children the opportunity to depict through artwork the idea that, even though kids can come from different countries, they all need the same things to survive and grow.
Description	Children create greeting cards based upon a theme. Guidelines are available in Pier 1 stores and on the website.
Eligibility	Students ages 14 and under.
Important Dates	Entries due in late November. See guidelines for specific dates.
How to Enter	See official contest rules for details.
Judging Criteria	Artistic quality and creative interpretation of the theme.
Judges	Officials from sponsoring organizations.
Winner Notification	Winners are notified in January.
Awards	The Grand Prize winner receives a $5,000 scholarship and $500 worth of art supplies donated to his or her school. The Fan's Choice winner received $500 worth of art supplies donated to his or her school. The two winning cards are printed by the U.S. Committee for UNICEF and sold exclusively at Pier 1 stores.

Competition	**President's Environmental Youth Awards**
Sponsor	U.S. Environmental Protection Agency 1200 Pennsylvania Ave., NW (1704A) Washington, DC 20460
Web Address	http://www.epa.gov/peya/
Areas	Science and service learning
Competition Origin	1971
Purpose	To offer young people an opportunity to become an environmental force within their communities.
Description	The program has two components: the regional certificate program and the national awards competition. Students are recognized for their efforts to make and keep the world around us a safer, cleaner place to live. Contact your regional EPA office for guidelines or look on the website.
Eligibility	Students in grades K–12.
Important Dates	Regional applications are accepted year-round; however, at the national level, applications must be submitted by December 31st.
How to Enter	Obtain an application and detailed guidelines from your regional EPA office or from the website.
Judging Criteria	The judging panel considers the following: environmental need for the project; environmental appropriateness of the project, accomplishment of goals, long–term environmental benefits derived from the project; positive environmental impact on the local community and society; evidence of the young person's initiative, innovation, soundness of approach, rationale, and scientific design (if applicable); and clarity and effectiveness of presentation.
Judges	Judging panel selected by the EPA.
Winner Notification	Dates vary for regional contests. National winners are notified in the fall.
Awards	All participants at the regional level receive certificates signed by the President of the United States honoring them for their efforts in environmental protection. The national winners, along with one project sponsor, receive an all-expense-paid trip to the National

Advice

Awards Ceremony and consult with the EPA Youth Work Group about the program.

For winning ideas, look at the past winners' projects on the website.

Competition	**Promising Young Writers Program**
Sponsor	National Council of Teachers of English 1111 W. Kenyon Road Urbana, IL 61801-1096
Web Address	http://www.ncte.org/awards/student/pyw
Area	Language arts
Competition Origin	1984
Purpose	To develop skills in writing.
Description	Students submit their best work and a themed essay that has been drafted and edited. Different genres should be used, including poetry, narrative, argument and exposition.
Eligibility	Students in grade 8 (must be nominated by their teachers).
Important Dates	Entries are accepted online from November to February. Visit the website for details.
How to Enter	Teachers complete a nomination form for each student nominee. This can be downloaded from the website or requested via mail.
Judging Criteria	Criteria include the content, purpose, audience, tone, word choice, organization, development, and style.
Judges	The entries are judged by teams of teachers.
Winner Notification	All certificates are mailed to school principals, who are asked to present them to each student who submitted writing samples. Nominating teachers will also be notified.
Awards	Each student who enters receives a citation. Certificates of recognition are awarded to students cited as winners. Certificates of participation are awarded to other nominees who write.
Advice	The number of nominees allowed from each school is determined by the school's average eighth-grade daily enrollment. Students should talk with their teachers about this competition.

Competition	**Prudential Spirit of Community Awards**
Sponsor	Prudential Spirit of Community Awards International Scholarship and Tuition Services 200 Crutchfield Avenue Nashville, TN 37210
Web Address	http://www.prudential.com/community/spirit
Areas	Leadership and service learning
Competition Origin	1995
Purpose	To recognize students in middle and high school grades who have demonstrated exemplary community service.
Description	Student applicants compete based upon descriptions of their community service projects, highlighting their leadership roles. Visit the website for guidelines.
Eligibility	Students in grades 5–12 who have engaged in a volunteer activity in the 12 months prior to the competition.
Important Dates	Student applications are due between late October and early November. See guidelines for specific dates.
How to Enter	Applications can be downloaded from the website. The application (a) must describe an individual community service activity or an individual's significant leadership in a group activity that has taken place during the previous year, (b) must be completed and submitted to a school principal or the head of an officially designated organization, and (c) must be certified by the principal of a middle-level or high school or the head of an officially designated local organization.
Judging Criteria	Judges consider students' initiative, effort, impact, and personal growth in assessing the applications.
Judges	A national board of prominent judges.
Winner Notification	State winners are notified in March; national winners are honored in May.
Awards	Local honorees receive a certificate of recognition from their schools or organizations. State honorees receive a beautifully engraved silver medallion, a monetary award of $1,000, and an all-expense-paid

trip with a parent or guardian to Washington, D.C., in early May for several days of recognition events. The medallion is presented in the State honoree's hometown by a local Prudential representative, and the $1,000 award is presented in Washington, DC.

Competition	**Questions Unlimited National Academic Championship**
Sponsor	National Academic Championship
Web Address	http://www.qunlimited.com/
Area	Academic Quiz Bowl
Competition Origin	1978
Purpose	To promote excellence in academics.
Description	The tournament consists of several rounds of academic questions. Students will compete in teams of four with substitutions allowed at the end of a round. There is a High School division and a Junior division. Nationals are held in three cities during the months of May and June.
Eligibility	High school and middle/junior high school students.
Important Dates	Deadline for entry is May 15, but early enrollment is recommended as there are limited spaces available.
How to Enter	Complete rules can be viewed on the website, where registration forms can also be found.
Judging Criteria	Judging is based on the most correct answers during each round.
Judges	Chip Beall, Brick Barrientos, Ernie Anderson, Jason Russell, Chris Hunter, Brooks Sanders, and Ariel Schieler.
Winner Notification	Winners are announced at the competition.
Awards	Plaques and trophies are presented to winning teams.
Advice	Check the website for updates and changes in deadlines, and to choose a competition site.

Competition	**Quill and Scroll Yearbook Excellence Contest**
Sponsor	Walsworth Yearbooks and the Quill and Scroll International Honorary Society
Web Address	http://quillandscroll.org/contests/ yearbook-excellence-contest
Area	Journalism and visual arts
Competition Origin	1926
Purpose	To promote scholastic journalism.
Description	A high school yearbook competition that includes 18 divisions. The divisions are Theme Development, Student Life, Academics, Clubs or Organizations, Sports, People, Advertising, Sports Action Photo, Academic Photo, Student Life Photo, Clubs or Organizations Photo, Feature Photo, Graphic Design, Photo Illustration, Index, Headline Writing and Design, Caption Writing, and Personality Profiles.
Eligibility	High school students who are contributors or staff members of their high school yearbook.
Important Dates	Deadline for entry is early November.
How to Enter	Students may enter through their school's charter with Quill and Pen. Charters are available to schools free of charge. Each school can have four entries per division except for the Theme division, which can only have one entry.
Judging Criteria	Each division will be judged on creativity and functionality.
Judges	Judges with expertise in all areas of journalism will evaluate the entries.
Winner Notification	Only winners will be notified and a list of winners will be posted online at Quill and Pen.
Awards	Winners will receive Quill and Scroll's National Award Gold Key and high school seniors will be eligible to apply for Edward J. Nell Memorial or George and Ophelia Gallup scholarships.
Advice	Check for updates on entry deadlines and additional categories.

Competition	**Quill and Scroll International Writing and Photo Contest**
Sponsor	Quill and Scroll Magazine
Web Address	http://quillandscroll.org/contests/ writing-photo-contest
Area	Journalism and visual arts
Competition Origin	1998
Purpose	To promote scholastic journalism.
Description	A journalism competition that includes written and photographic entries.
Eligibility	Entrants for this competition must have been published in a public or school publication, either online or in print, between February 1 of the current year and February 1 of the previous year. There are two age divisions, High School and Middle/Junior High School.
Important Dates	Deadline for entry is early February.
How to Enter	Students may enter through your school's charter with Quill and Pen. Only four applicants per division are allowed from each school. Charters are free of charge and may be applied for by the journalism teacher or advisor at your school. An entry form is required.
Judging Criteria	Writings should be well written and factual.
Judges	Experts in journalism.
Winner Notification	Only winners will be notified and a list of winners will be posted online at Quill and Pen.
Awards	Winners will receive Quill and Scroll's National Award Gold Key and high school seniors will be eligible to apply for scholarships offered by Quill and Scroll.
Advice	Check for updates on entry deadlines and additional categories.

Competition	**Reconnecting the Circle Essay Contest**
Sponsor	Reconnecting the Circle, Inc.
Web Address	http://www.reconnectingthecircle.com/essay-contest/
Area	Language arts
Competition Origin	2006
Purpose	To encourage people of all backgrounds to learn about Native American people and their cultures.
Description	Students write a 750–1,200 word essay answering the year's essay topic.
Eligibility	Students in grades 9–12
Important Dates	Essays may be entered online between November 1 and February 22.
How to Enter	Enter online through the website.
Judging Criteria	Entries are judged based on ideas and content, organization, voice, word choice, sentence fluency, conventions, and the appropriate citing of sources.
Judges	Entries will be judged by a panel of reviewers selected by Reconnecting The Circle, Inc.
Winner Notification	Winners will be notified by the contact information provided on the Contestant's Official Entry Form.
Awards	Up to 10 winners will each receive a $2,500 scholarship and the opportunity to have their winning essays listed on the website.
Advice	Check the website for the current essay question and updates of deadlines.

Competition	**River of Words Youth Environmental Poetry and Art Contest**
Sponsor	River of Words P.O. Box 5060 Moraga, CA 94575-5060
Web Address	http://www.stmarys-ca.edu/ center-for-environmental-literacy/river-of-words
Area	Language arts and visual arts
Competition Origin	1995
Purpose	To encourage children of all ages to explore their local watershed and then create poetry and/or art about what was observed.
Description	Children submit their original poetry or artwork about the place they live and particularly their watersheds.
Eligibility	Individual or group entries for all grade levels (ages 5–19), nationally and internationally.
Important Dates	National entries are due by December 1. International entries must be received by February 1.
How to Enter	The entry form is available on the website. A separate form must be completed for each entry, and there are individual and school entry forms. Original poetry should not exceed 32 lines. Artwork must not exceed 11 inches by 17 inches, but can be created with any acceptable media (paint, pencil, marker, ink, crayon, chalk, pastel, cloth, collage, photography, or computer art).
Judging Criteria	Written entries must be legible and in English, Spanish, or American Sign Language. Collaborative poems are accepted, but only one child (i.e., the group representative) will be eligible for any prizes awarded. All works must be original.
Judges	The sponsor selects winning entries.
Winner Notification	Winners are announced in April each year.
Awards	The grand-prize winner receives round-trip transportation for him or herself and one parent or guardian from the winner's nearest major airport to

the city where the Grand Prize Ceremony is being held.

Advice

All submissions become the property of River of Words, with non-exclusive reproduction and publication rights to the works submitted, which will not be returned.

Competition	**Reflections Cultural Arts Program**
Sponsor	National PTA 330 N. Wabash Ave., Suite 2100 Chicago, IL 60611
Web Address	http://pta.org/programs/ArtsandEducation.cfm?navItemNumber=510
Areas	Language arts, performing arts, and visual arts
Competition Origin	1969
Purpose	To provide opportunities for students to express and share their creative abilities. Each year, works of art are inspired by a theme, which is chosen from hundreds of student theme entries.
Description	There are six arts categories: dance choreography, film production, literature, musical composition, photography, and visual arts. Students may enter the National PTA Reflections Program in one or more arts categories.
Eligibility	Students in grades Pre-K–12. There are four grade divisions: Primary (Pre-K–2), Intermediate (3–5), Middle/Junior (6–8), and Senior (9–12). Any PTA/PTSA in good standing may sponsor the Reflections Program.
Important Dates	Contact your state PTA for dates.
How to Enter	See guidelines for details.
Judging Criteria	All national entries are judged on interpretation of the theme, artistic merit, creative merit, and technical merit.
Judges	Professionals working in literature, musical composition, photography, and visual arts fields volunteer to judge student entries at the national level.
Winner Notification	All state PTAs are notified of national award recipients in late April and National PTA sends award notification letters directly to students.
Awards	Three Awards of Excellence and five Awards of Merit are selected in each grade division for each of the arts areas. In addition, one national Outstanding Interpretation work is chosen from among the Awards of Excellence in each arts area. These students

receive a trip to National PTA's Annual Convention for themselves and one adult chaperone. At the convention, the Outstanding Interpretation award recipients are recognized for their achievement and share their talents at a special awards presentation.

Advice

Each entry must be the work of one student. Each student and his or her parent or guardian must sign the affirmation sentence on the official entry form stating that the entry is original. Artwork may be created in or outside of school.

Competition	**The Scholastic Student Journalism Contest**
Sponsor	The Association of Educational Publishers
Web Address	http://www.aepweb.org/aepweb/index.php/awards/student-journalism-contest.html
Area	Journalism
Competition Origin	1923
Purpose	To promote nonfiction writing.
Description	Students submit 500–2,500-word writing pieces or whole publication entries in a journalism format.
Eligibility	Students in grades 3–12.
Important Dates	The deadline for entry is March 15.
How to Enter	Complete rules and the entry form can be downloaded from the website.
Judging Criteria	Writing technique, topic, and accuracy are essential elements for the winning submission.
Judges	Judges will be knowledgeable in publishing and journalism.
Winner Notification	Winners will be honored at the annual Association of Educational Publishers' luncheon in Washington, DC.
Awards	Winners receive round-trip travel and accommodations to Washington, DC, for themselves, a teacher adviser, and a parent; a $250 Scholastic Store gift voucher and a SMART Board for their school; and recognition on the Scholastic website.
Advice	Check the website for updates to deadlines and contest rules.

Competition	**Scholastic Art & Writing Awards**
Sponsor	Scholastic Art & Writing Awards 557 Broadway New York, NY 10012
Web Address	http://www.artandwriting.org
Areas	Language arts and visual arts
Competition Origin	1923
Purpose	To recognize and encourage outstanding writing and artwork by students.
Description	This is the nation's largest, longest running, and most prestigious recognition program for young artists and writers. There are a variety of competitions available for students. Check the website in October for new guidelines and deadlines.
Eligibility	Students in grades 7–12. The portfolio competitions are for graduating seniors.
Important Dates	Check the website for the latest competition details.
How to Enter	You can obtain an entry form online or by writing to the sponsor.
Judging Criteria	Writing awards are based upon technical proficiency, style, emergence of writer's voice, and originality. Art awards vary with each competition.
Judges	Panels of qualified writers, editors, and educators.
Winner Notification	Varies with each competition.
Awards	More than 600 art awards and 300 writing awards are presented annually on the national level. Winners may receive cash awards, scholarships, certificates, and publishing and exhibition opportunities.
Advice	Originality is essential to winning. Be sure to check the website for details for each competition in your region, as deadlines and requirements vary.

Competition	**Science Olympiad**
Sponsor	Science Olympiad 2 Trans Am Plaza Drive, Suite 415 Oakbrook Terrace, Illinois 60181
Web Address	http://www.soinc.org
Areas	Mathematics, science, and technology
Competition Origin	1984
Purpose	To challenge students to reach for higher goals and aspirations; to increase the interest of precollege students in science, mathematics, and technology so that high-tech careers are an option as the students matriculate into institutions of higher education; and to wrap these serious intents into a context of a fun, exciting activity.
Description	The Science Olympiad is an international nonprofit organization devoted to improving the quality of science education, increasing student interest in science, and providing recognition for outstanding achievement in science education by both students and teachers. The Science Olympiad tournaments are rigorous academic, interscholastic competitions that consist of a series of 23 team events, which students prepare for during the year. The competitions follow the format of popular board games, TV shows, and athletic games. The Rules Manual and Coaches Handbooks are available from the national offices or can be downloaded online.
Eligibility	Students in grades K–12. The Olympiad has four grade divisions: A1 (K–3); A2 (3–6); B (6–9); and C (9–12). Only Divisions B and C have state, regional, and national competitions. Division A (A1 or A2) has only local or district activities.
Important Dates	Each local, district, county, and state sets its own dates for competitions. The National Tournament is generally held during the third weekend in May. Since attendance at the National Tournament requires placement at state tournaments, states generally hold their competitions no later than mid-April. See guidelines for specific dates.
How to Enter	Contact the national office for advice on registering.

Judging Criteria | Judging criteria vary from event to event.

Judges | Each tournament site is responsible for finding local judges with the technical expertise to judge the activity. This is the reason that many tournaments are held at college or university sites.

Winner Notification | At all tournaments an awards ceremony is held and winners are named.

Awards | Trophies are given to schools, winning coaches get plaques, and students receive Olympic-style medals.

Competition	**Scripps National Spelling Bee**
Sponsor	Scripps National Spelling Bee 312 Walnut St., 28th Floor Cincinnati, OH 45202
Web Address	http://www.spellingbee.com
Area	Language arts
Competition Origin	1925
Purpose	To help students improve their spelling, increase their vocabularies, acquire concepts, learn language development, and improve reading skills that will benefit them their entire lives.
Description	The program takes place on two levels: local and national. The only way students may participate in the National Spelling Bee is through an authorized sponsor in their area. The majority of sponsors are either daily, weekly, or Sunday newspapers. Authorized sponsors organize programs in their locales, often in cooperation with educators, businesses, and community organizations. These sponsors send their champions to the national finals. Guidelines may be obtained on the website or by writing to the sponsor.
Eligibility	Students in grade 8 and under.
Important Dates	The 2-day national competition is held on Wednesday and Thursday during the week of Memorial Day. See guidelines for specific dates.
How to Enter	Contact the local authorized sponsor.
Judging Criteria	The Scripps National Spelling Bee is an oral competition conducted in rounds until only one speller remains. Each speller has been assigned a number and will spell in this order. A speller who correctly spells his or her word stays seated on the stage and waits for the next round. If the speller misspells his or her given word, that speller is eliminated from the competition.
Judges	Appointed at local and national level by sponsors.
Winner Notification	Winners are announced upon completion of each level of competition.

Awards

The first-place winner receives a $12,000 cash prize and an engraved loving cup trophy from the E. W. Scripps Company, choice of the Anniversary Edition of the *New Encyclopedia Britannica* or the *Great Books of the Western World* from Encyclopedia Britannica, and a $1,000 U.S. savings bond from Merriam-Webster. The second-place prize is $5,000, and the third-place prize is $3,500.

Competition	**SeaWorld Environmental Educator of the Year Award**
Sponsor	SeaWorld Parks & Entertainment SeaWorld Orlando Education Department 7007 SeaWorld Drive Orlando, FL 32821
Web Address	http://seaworldparks.com/en/SeaWorld_Teachers/ Environmental-Excellence-Awards
Area	Science and service learning
Competition Origin	1993
Purpose	To recognize an outstanding environmental educator (youth or adult) who has made a significant impact on the environment.
Description	Students nominate an environmental hero by producing an original video
Eligibility	Open to nominees of all ages.
Important Dates	The deadline for entry is early March.
How to Enter	Create a video nominating an environmental hero and post it on YouTube, then mail the link to buschgardenseducation@gmail.com.
Judging Criteria	Nominees are selected at the discretion of SeaWorld and Busch Gardens. Make sure your video answers the following questions about the nominee for the award: Why should this person be selected as an Environmental Excellence Award winner? What are the most significant positive impacts the nominee has made? If your nominee is selected as a winner, how will that help them to make a bigger impact on the environment? How does the nominee inspire others and why are you personally nominating this person?
Judges	The Education Department of SeaWorld and Busch Gardens.
Winner Notification	Winners are announced on the website.
Awards	The winner receives $10,000 and an all-expense-paid trip to the National Science Teachers Association Conference, where he or she will be honored at an awards banquet.

Advice

Please note that this is a competition requiring nomination by another individual who recognizes your contributions to environmental excellence.

Competition	*Skipping Stones* **Youth Honor Award Program**
Sponsor	*Skipping Stones* magazine P.O. Box 3939 Eugene, OR 97403
Web Address	http://www.skippingstones.org/youthhonor-02.htm
Area	Language arts
Competition Origin	1989
Purpose	To promote multicultural, international understanding, and nature awareness.
Description	Students are to produce an original piece of writing (e.g., essay, play, poem, short story) that highlights multicultural awareness, international understanding, or nature awareness. Non-English or bilingual entries are accepted.
Eligibility	Students ages 7–17
Important Dates	The deadline for entry is June 25.
How to Enter	Entries should be neatly handwritten or typed. Include a cover letter with your name, address, telephone, email, and age. A letter from a teacher or parent confirming originality must be included with your entry. If you would like your writing returned, include a stamped, self-addressed envelope. Poems should not exceed 30 lines and prose should be fewer than 1,000 words. Accompanying artwork is encouraged. Mail entries to *Skipping Stones* magazine or electronically submit to Info@SkippingStones.org.
Judging Criteria	Winning entries will be original and well written.
Judges	Judges will be knowledgeable in literature and writing.
Winner Notification	10 winners will be published in a fall edition of *Stepping Stones* magazine.
Awards	Award certificates will be issued to the winners along with a one-year subscription to *Stepping Stones* magazine and five nature and/or multicultural books. Winners will also be asked to join the magazine's Student Review Board.
Advice	Check the website for changes to submission dates as well as to see what other contests are currently being offered by *Stepping Stones* magazine. The website also gives information about submitting material for publication to the magazine.

Competition	**Smokey Bear/Woodsy Owl Poster Contest**
Sponsor	National Garden Clubs, Inc. and the U.S. Department of Agriculture Forest Service
Web Address	http://www.gardenclub.org/youth/contests/smokey-bear-poster-contest.aspx
Area	Visual arts and service learning
Competition Origin	1961
Purpose	To prevent forest fires and conserve natural resources.
Description	Students will enter original posters depicting Smokey Bear or Woodsy Owl.
Eligibility	Students in grades 1–5
Important Dates	Local deadlines are in late January, and State Garden Clubs must submit entries to the regional contest by mid-February. See the website for specific dates.
How to Enter	Enter a poster depicting Smokey the Bear including a slogan to prevent forest fires or Woodsy Owl with a slogan to save our land through a local garden club contest.
Judging Criteria	Posters will be judged on originality, design, slogan, artwork, and overall effectiveness of the message.
Judges	Judges will be familiar with the characters depicted in the posters and/or in art.
Winner Notification	National winners and the Grand National winner will be announced at the National Garden Clubs, Inc. Annual Meeting.
Awards	The National Grand Prize Winner of the Smokey Bear & Woodsy Owl Poster Contest will be honored with a Recognition Ceremony in Washington, DC. Round-trip airfare and accommodations for four will be provided. In addition, National Garden Clubs, Inc. will award $50 to the first-place winner for each grade level category.
Advice	Check the website for updates in rules and deadlines as well as for links to complete rules and local Garden Clubs.

Competition	**Student Electronic Music Composition Talent Search**
Sponsor	National Association for Music Education (NAfME) 1806 Robert Fulton Dr. Reston, VA 20901
Web Address	http://musiced.nafme.org/programs/ contests-calls-competitions/ nafme-electronic-music-composition-contest
Area	Performing arts
Competition Origin	2002
Purpose	To recognize outstanding electronic music composition.
Description	Teachers must submit an original student composition of 5 minutes or less. Compositions must be written with the use of electronic instrument(s) or other electronic media for manipulating sound, alone or with any combination of vocal and/or acoustic instruments, live or recorded. Auxiliary support materials must be limited to one of the following: a video no longer than 5 minutes, an essay no longer than 1,000 words, or a PowerPoint presentation printout of fewer than 30 slides. Composition must be part of a classroom curriculum and correspond to relevant standards. Visit the website to download guidelines and an application.
Eligibility	Students in grades K–12. There are three grade divisions: Elementary (K–5); Middle level (6–8); and High School (grades 9–12).
Important Dates	Entries are due in mid-April. See guidelines for specific dates.
How to Enter	Download an entry form from the website and follow the instructions carefully. You must be sponsored by a NAfME member teacher, and your teacher must enter the composition on your behalf.
Judging Criteria	Aesthetic quality, effective use of electronic media, and the power of the composition and its presentation in communicating to school board members, administrators, and others the excitement and effectiveness of electronic music composition in the school curriculum.

Judges	Members of the National Association for Music Education.
Winner Notification	Winners are posted on the website in July.
Awards	Winners and their schools receive varying prizes from sponsors.
Advice	Past winners' compositions are on the website. Note that there is an entry fee of $15.

Competition	**TEAMS (Tests of Engineering Aptitude, Mathematics, and Science)**
Sponsor	Technology Student Association (TSA) 1914 Association Drive Reston, VA 20191-1540
Web Address	http://teams.tsaweb.org/
Areas	Engineering, mathematics, and science
Competition Origin	1979
Purpose	To help prepare students for tomorrow's world today.
Description	Teams participate in an open-book, open-discussion environment to solve real-world engineering problems. Mathematics and science concepts taught in school are applied to real-world problems. TEAMS problems focus on all areas of mathematics and science, as well as on computer fundamentals, graphics interpretation, and English/communication skills and concepts. Information is updated each summer for the following year's TEAMS program. Information is available year-round from the sponsor or on the website.
Eligibility	There are high school (9–12) and middle school (6–8) divisions.
Important Dates	TEAMS is a 1-day, two-part event held in June or July each year. Schools may register teams beginning in September. See guidelines for specific dates.
How to Enter	Schools that have not participated before should contact TSA for information on the competition site nearest them. All schools register directly with the competition host.
Judging Criteria	Part 1 (multiple-choice) is scored based on the accuracy of answers. Part 2 (subjective portion) is scored by a panel of engineers.
Judges	The objective test is machine scored. Engineers and coordinators judge the subjective portion.
Winner Notification	Teams usually receive local (regional) results on competition day.

Awards   Awards are given for regional, state, and national
recognition. Regional and state awards vary by site
and state; national awards vary from year to year.

Advice   The website has some good support materials, as well
as monthly math challenges.

the best competitions for talented kids

Competition	**ThinkQuest Competition**
Sponsor	Oracle Education Foundation 500 Oracle Parkway, MS 1 LGN-2 Redwood Shores, CA 94065
Web Address	http://www.thinkquest.org
Area	Technology
Competition Origin	2003
Purpose	To challenge students to be creative and original.
Description	Students build a ThinkQuest project, create a digital media response to a problem (online journal/blog, standalone website, photo essay, animation, public service announcement, video or some combination of these items), or develop an application for an interactive application or game.
Eligibility	Students ages 9–19
Important Dates	Students upload webpages in mid-March for peer review in April. Final modifications are made in late April and judging takes place in May. See guidelines for specific dates.
How to Enter	Teachers may enroll through the competition website as a coach. The students may also enter the contest through the website.
Judging Criteria	The students' website is judged on educational content, design, and community. A rubric is featured on the website.
Judges	There is a peer review process, followed by modifications before final judging by an international panel of education specialists.
Winner Notification	Winners are notified at the end of May.
Awards	The winning websites become part of the ThinkQuest Library. First-place winners receive a laptop computer with approximate retail value of $1,500, a trip to ThinkQuest Live, and a $5,000 School Award.
Advice	Previous years' winning entries can be viewed at the website.

Competition	**Toshiba/NSTA ExploraVision Awards Program**
Sponsor	Toshiba and the National Science Teachers Association (NSTA) 1840 Wilson Blvd. Arlington, VA 22201-3000
Web Address	http://www.exploravision.org
Area	Technology and science
Competition Origin	1992
Purpose	To provide opportunities for K–12 students to enhance or design technologies that could exist in the future.
Description	This is the world's largest science contest in which teams of three to four students in grades K–12 expand on or design technologies that could exist 20 years in the future. Guidelines may be obtained on the website or by writing to the sponsor.
Eligibility	Students in grades K–12. There are four grade divisions: K–3, 4–6, 7–9, and 10–12.
Important Dates	The entry deadline is in late January. The regional winners are announced in February. The finalists are announced in early May and the awards ceremony is in June. See guidelines for specific dates.
How to Enter	Teams submit a project that includes an abstract, a description, a bibliography, and five sample web pages.
Judging Criteria	Decisions are based upon creativity, scientific accuracy, communication, and feasibility of vision.
Judges	Leading science educators serve as judges.
Winner Notification	The eight finalists of the national competition are notified in early May. The four first-place winners will be notified during ExploraVision Awards Weekend in early June.
Awards	Student members of the four first-place teams each receive a U.S. EE savings bond worth $10,000 at maturity. Second-place winners receive U.S. EE series bonds worth $5,000 at maturity. National finalist team members and their parents/guardians travel to Washington, DC, in June for ExploraVision

Awards Weekend, where they are recognized for their outstanding achievement. Each student on the 24 regional winning teams and honorable mention teams is recognized for his or her creative vision with a special gift. Every student team member who enters the competition with a complete entry receives a certificate of participation and a small gift. There are also prizes and recognition for coaches and mentors.

Advice

The website answers many questions students may have and is filled with useful information.

Competition	**United States Academic Triathlon**
Sponsor	U.S. Academic Triathlon
Web Address	http://www.academictriathlon.org
Area	Creativity/problem solving
Competition Origin	1989
Purpose	To promote creative thinking and problem solving.
Description	U.S. Academic Triathlon features three events to test creative thinking and problem-solving abilities. This is a team competition and consists of five-member teams plus alternates.
Eligibility	Students in grades 5–8
Important Dates	Registration dates are May 15–October 24.
How to Enter	Complete rules and regulations can be found at the website.
Judging Criteria	Winners will be determined by best scores of the three divisions of competition.
Judges	Team coaches are responsible for keeping accurate scores of the rounds of competition. A program facilitator insures that all rules are being followed.
Winner Notification	Winners will be announced at the event.
Awards	Team members receive certificates of participation and ribbons.
Advice	Check all rules and regulations as well as deadlines for changes.

the best competitions for talented kids

Competition	**United States Senate Youth Program**
Sponsor	William Randolph Hearst Foundation 90 New Montgomery St. #1212 San Francisco, CA 94105-4504
Web Address	http://www.hearstfdn.org/ussyp
Areas	Leadership, service learning, and social studies
Competition Origin	1962
Purpose	To encourage leadership qualities and an interest in government and community service.
Description	Two student leaders from each state, the District of Columbia, and the Department of Defense Education Activity spend a week in Washington, DC, experiencing their national government in action. Guidelines may be obtained on the website or by writing to the sponsor.
Eligibility	Students in grades 11–12 who are currently serving as elected student body officers.
Important Dates	Deadlines vary by state, but are usually in the fall. See guidelines for specific dates.
How to Enter	Contact your high school principal, state Department of Education, or the foundation for information.
Judging Criteria	Varies by state.
Judges	Appointed by each state Department of Education.
Winner Notification	Generally, winners are notified in December.
Awards	Winners receive a $5,000 college scholarship and an all-expense-paid week in Washington, DC, where they will learn about government organizations.
Advice	Students should start exploring participation in this program soon after the school year begins.

Competition	**U.S. Academic Decathlon**
Sponsor	U.S. Academic Decathlon P.O. Box 1834 Council Bluffs, IA 51502-1834
Web Address	http://www.usad.org
Area	Academic quiz bowl
Competition Origin	1981
Purpose	To improve the status, the recognition, and the popularity of academic endeavors in every high school in the U.S.
Description	The Academic Decathlon is a 10-event scholastic competition for teams of high school students. Guidelines may be obtained on the website or by writing to the sponsor.
Eligibility	Students in grades 9–12. Each high school enters a team of nine students: three "A" or Honor students; three "B" or Scholastic students; and three "C" or Varsity students.
Important Dates	Local and state competitions are held prior to the national finals in April. See guidelines for specific dates.
How to Enter	See the website for details.
Judging Criteria	Accuracy of answers.
Judges	Volunteers and company personnel manage the process of scoring.
Winner Notification	Winners are notified at the national finals in April.
Awards	Gold, silver, and bronze medals are awarded for individual events and total scores.
Advice	Study materials and resource guides are available for purchase on the website. It is important to contact local and state sponsors to ensure that deadlines are met for participation.

Competition	**U.S. National Chemistry Olympiad**
Sponsor	American Chemical Society 1155 16th St. NW Washington, DC 20036
Web Address	http://portal.acs.org/portal/acs/corg/content
Area	Science
Competition Origin	1984
Purpose	To promote excellence in chemistry, as well as to select four students to represent the United States at the International Chemistry Olympiad.
Description	The U.S. National Chemistry Olympiad (USNCO) is a multi-tiered competition for high school students. The local section competitions are usually held from late February to early April and consist of a locally determined competition such as a written exam, a laboratory practical, or a science fair. The best students from the local competition participate in the three-part national exam in late April. The national exam consists of a 60-question multiple-choice section, an eight-question free-response section, and a two-exercise laboratory practical. Guidelines may be obtained on the website or by writing to the sponsor.
Eligibility	Students in grades 9–12 who are enrolled in chemistry.
Important Dates	Local competitions are held February through April, and the national exam is given in late April. See guidelines for specific dates.
How to Enter	Students should discuss entry with their chemistry teacher, who can register by contacting the sponsor.
Judging Criteria	Accuracy of answers.
Judges	Teachers and chemists.
Winner Notification	Winners are announced on-site for national and international competitions.
Awards	Of the approximately 1,000 students taking this exam, 20 are invited to attend a 2-week study camp held at the U.S. Air Force Academy in mid-June. At the study camp, the students undergo an intense schedule of lectures, laboratory exercises, and exams. The top four students are selected from the camp to compete in the International Chemistry Olympiad in July.

Competition	**USA Biology Olympiad (USABO)**
Sponsor	Center for Excellence in Education 8201 Greensboro Dr., Suite 215 McLean, VA 22102
Web Address	http://www.usabo-trc.org/
Area	Science
Competition Origin	1960s
Purpose	To motivate high school students' curiosity about the different fields of biology. This competition also focuses on challenging students and allowing them to experience competitive opportunities.
Description	This is a four-level competition that consists of multiple-choice questions, short answers, and group competitions. Teachers begin by registering their biology class. This can be done through the USABO website. Guidelines are sent after this step is completed.
Eligibility	Students in grades 9–12 who are enrolled in biology.
Important Dates	Registration is from November to January. The open exam is in January and the semifinals will be held in March. The fourth round of the competition is held in mid-July. See guidelines for specific dates.
How to Enter	Have your biology teacher visit the website and register your class.
Judging Criteria	Accuracy of answers.
Judges	Teachers and USABO officials.
Winner Notification	Winners are notified at each level of competition.
Awards	The top 20 scorers on the Semifinal Exam advance to the National Finals. The top four at this level advance to the International Biology Olympiad. Medals are also awarded.
Advice	The website offers sample exams linked to other websites. There are also other textbook listings and material provided for studying.

Competition	**USA Computing Olympiad (USACO)**
Sponsors	Clemson University School of Computing 100 McAdams Hall Clemson, SC 29634
Web Address	http://www.usaco.org
Areas	Creativity/problem solving and technology
Competition Origin	1992
Purpose	To select the team of four students to represent the United States in the annual International Olympiad in Informatics (IOI).
Description	The goals of the USACO are to provide U.S. students with opportunities to sharpen their computing skills, enabling them to compete successfully at the international level; enhance the quality of computer education in U.S. high schools by providing students and teachers with challenging programming problems that emphasize algorithm development and problem-solving skills; and select the U.S. team to attend the annual International Olympiad in Informatics. Students progress through a number of rounds in which they must successfully answer different programming problems. Information about the USACO and IOI is available on the website.
Eligibility	Students in grades 6–12.
Important Dates	Contests are held in November, December, January, February, and March, with the national competition in April. See guidelines for specific dates.
How to Enter	Contact a high school or college teacher who will serve as a local coordinator. Have the local coordinator contact the USACO or sign up online at the website.
Judging Criteria	The winners are selected based on their performance at the final round of the USACO.
Judges	USACO staff members serve as judges.
Winner Notification	The USA team is notified at the April competition.
Awards	The 16 finalists in the Competition Round receive an all-expenses-paid trip to a weeklong training camp. Four students selected for the USACO team receive an all-expenses-paid trip to the International Olympiad in Informatics, which is held in a different country each year and lasts for 10 days.

Competition	**USA Mathematical Talent Search (USAMTS)**
Sponsor	USA Mathematical Talent Search P.O. Box 2090 Alpine, CA 91903-2090
Web Address	http://www.usamts.org
Area	Mathematics
Competition Origin	1989
Purpose	To encourage and assist the development of problem solving skills of talented high school students.
Description	Most competitions require students to answer several questions over a few hours, often in multiple-choice format. The USAMTS is different in that students have a full month to work out their solutions. Carefully written justifications are required for each problem. Each year, the USAMTS consists of four rounds, each round featuring five problems. The problems are published on the USAMTS website. Each round of problems is published to allow at least 4 weeks for solution. Students are asked to submit solutions to at least two of the problems each round. They can earn 5 points for the complete, well-written solution of each problem, and hence can accumulate 100 points during the school year. Guidelines may be obtained on the website or by writing to the sponsor.
Eligibility	Students in grades 6–12.
Important Dates	Solutions are due in early October, November, January, and March. Check the website for dates. See guidelines for specific dates.
How to Enter	Visit the website for details and your entry application.
Judging Criteria	Accuracy of answers.
Judges	USAMTS officials.
Winner Notification	At the end of each round, in addition to the solutions and a copy of the completed individual USAMTS cover sheet, each participant receives a copy of a newsletter, which provides an update on the competition, as well as other valuable information.
Awards	Certificates and book prizes are given to gold, silver, and bronze winners, and prizes are given for honorable mention winners.

Competition	**The Vegetarian Resource Group's Annual Essay Contest**
Sponsor	The Vegetarian Resource Group P.O. Box 1463 Baltimore, MD 21203
Web Address	http://www.vrg.org/essay
Area	Language arts
Competition Origin	1996
Purpose	To emphasize the ethics, culture, health, aesthetics, economics, and environmental issues that are involved with vegetarianism.
Description	Students write a 2–3 page essay on any issue related to vegetarianism. Guidelines are available through the website.
Eligibility	Students in grades K–12. There are three age divisions: 8 and under, 9–13, and 14–18.
Important Dates	Entries must be postmarked by early May. See guidelines for specific dates.
How to Enter	Mail essay to the sponsor's address or e-mail from the website.
Judging Criteria	Entries are judged based on personal opinion, research, and interviews.
Judges	Staff of The Vegetarian Resource Group.
Winner Notification	Winners are notified by mail upon completion of judging.
Awards	A $50 savings bond is awarded to the winner in each age division. The winning essays are also posted on the website.
Advice	You need not be a vegetarian to enter. All essays become the property of The Vegetarian Resource Group.

Competition	**VSA Playwright Discovery Competition**
Sponsor	Department of VSA and Accessibility at the John F. Kennedy Center for the Performing Arts 2700 F Street, NW Washington, DC 20566
Web Address	http://www.kennedy-center.org/education/vsa/programs/playwright_discovery.cfm
Areas	Language arts and performing arts
Competition Origin	2002
Purpose	To challenge middle and high school students of all abilities to take a closer look at the world around them, examine how disability affects their lives and the lives of others, and express their views through the art of writing a one-act play.
Description	Students write a one-act play that expresses how disability affects their lives and the lives of others. Guidelines may be obtained on the website or by writing to the sponsor.
Eligibility	Students in grades 6–12, regardless of ability. Students in grades 6–8 compete in Division 1, and students in grades 9–12 compete in Division 2. Submissions can be created individually or collaboratively.
Important Dates	Plays should be submitted by June 1.
How to Enter	Apply online or contact the organization for an application form.
Judging Criteria	Scripts must somehow address the issue of disability. The disability may be visible (e.g., a character who is blind or uses a wheelchair) or hidden (e.g., a character with a learning or emotional disability). Submissions must be appropriate in language and subject matter for middle and high school audiences.
Judges	A distinguished jury of award-winning theater professionals selects the winning scripts.
Winner Notification	Winners are notified prior to the awards recognition ceremony, which is held in September or October each year.
Awards	The Division 1 winner receives $375 for his/her school and the winning script is published in the VSA

Playwright Discovery Program booklet. The Division 2 winner receives a $750 scholarship, $375 for his/her school, and the winning script is published in the VSA Playwright Discovery Program booklet.

Competition	**VSA International Young Soloists Award**
Sponsor	Department of VSA and Accessibility at the John F. Kennedy Center for the Performing Arts 2700 F Street, NW Washington, DC 20566
Web Address	http://www.kennedy-center.org/education/vsa/programs/soloists_award.cfm
Area	Performing arts
Competition Origin	1984
Purpose	To recognize exceptional young musicians with disabilities.
Description	Applicants are required to complete an application form and submit a one-page personal narrative as well as three audio or video recordings. Contact the sponsor for guidelines or download them from the website.
Eligibility	Musically talented students ages 14–25 with a disability may enter as a domestic or international competitor. The competition is open to individuals or ensembles of up to five.
Important Dates	Entries are due in January. See guidelines for specific dates.
How to Enter	Request an application packet from the sponsor or download it from the website.
Judging Criteria	Technique, tone, intonation (if applicable), rhythm, and interpretation.
Judges	Professional musicians and music educators.
Winner Notification	Winners are notified in March.
Awards	Winners receive $2,500, professional development opportunities, and a performance at the John F. Kennedy Center for the Performing Arts in Washington, DC.

Competition	**Voice of Democracy**
Sponsor	The Veterans of Foreign Wars of the United States (VFW) & Ladies Auxiliary VFW Building 406 W. 34th St. Kansas City, MO 06411
Web Address	http://www.vfw.org/Community/Voice-of-Democracy
Area	Language arts
Competition Origin	1946
Purpose	To allow students the opportunity to voice opinions on a patriotic theme.
Description	Students compete for prizes and money with winners selected based upon an audio essay. This is an essay recorded on a CD as read by the student. The theme of the essay contest varies each year. Contact the local VFW Post or Auxiliary for guidelines or visit the website.
Eligibility	Students in grades 9–12.
Important Dates	Entry deadline is in early November. See guidelines for specific dates.
How to Enter	Contact sponsor for official rules. The website includes guidelines for entry and an entry form that can be downloaded.
Judging Criteria	Originality, content, and delivery.
Judges	Judges are selected by VFW and include representatives from the major broadcast networks and government officials.
Winner Notification	Winners are announced in March at the annual Veterans of Foreign Wars Washington Conference.
Awards	One winner for every 15 entries from the local (Post) level advances to the District level, and one winner per District advances to the state (Department) competition. The Department's first-place winner receives an all-expenses-paid trip to Washington, DC, plus the opportunity to compete for national scholarships. The first-place national winner receives a $30,000 scholarship.
Advice	Carefully read guidelines for details.

Competition	**Washington Crossing Foundation National Scholarship Awards**
Sponsor	Washington Crossing Foundation P.O. Box 503 Levittown, PA 19058
Web Address	www.gwcf.org
Area	Social studies
Competition Origin	1969
Purpose	To provide students who are planning careers in government service an opportunity to express their career plans.
Description	Each interested student is invited to write a one-page essay stating why he or she plans a career in government service. The student should include mention of any inspiration derived from the leadership of George Washington in his famous crossing of the Delaware. Applications are sent to all high schools in the United States in September each year. Details are also available on the website.
Eligibility	Students in grade 12 who are interested in going into government work.
Important Dates	Applications must be submitted to the foundation by mid-January. See guidelines for specific dates.
How to Enter	Request an application from the Washington Crossing Foundation or download the information from the website.
Judging Criteria	The judges' decision will be based on understanding of career requirements, purpose in choice of a career, qualities of leadership exhibited, sincerity, and historical perspective. Semifinalists may be interviewed by telephone as part of the selection process. All finalists will be interviewed by telephone.
Judges	The board of judges consists of at least three trustees of the Foundation, one member of the Washington Crossing Park Commission, and a prominent educator.
Winner Notification	Winners will be notified by telephone in April, with confirmation by mail.

Awards

There are several $5,000 scholarships awarded. Each award is paid over a period of 4 years, if the student meets the requirements of the college chosen, maintains a suitable scholastic level, and continues his or her career objective. Other state and regional awards may be available.

Advice

Applicants with full 4-year tuition scholarships are only eligible for 1-year special awards.

Competition	**We the People: The Citizen and the Constitution**
Sponsor	Center for Civic Education 5145 Douglas Fir Rd. Calabasas, CA 91302-1440
Web Address	http://www.civiced.org/programs/wtp
Area	Social studies
Competition Origin	1987
Purpose	To promote civic competence and responsibility among students.
Description	Upon completion of the curriculum, teachers involve their entire class in a simulated congressional hearing. A model of performance assessment, the hearing provides an excellent culminating activity and an opportunity for students to demonstrate their knowledge and understanding of the principles of the Constitution and Bill of Rights. Information may be obtained on the website or by writing to the sponsor.
Eligibility	Classes in grades 9–12.
Important Dates	Interested teachers contact the coordinator for the congressional district their school is in and request instructional material in August or September. District-level hearings are held in November–January. State-level hearings are held in January–March, and the national-level hearings are held in April or May. See guidelines for specific dates.
How to Enter	Have your teacher contact the Center for Civic Education and request the name of the state and district coordinator for the congressional district in which your school is located.
Judging Criteria	At the district level, the judges score the students' performance on the basis of their knowledge and understanding of the Constitution and Bill of Rights and their ability to apply constitutional principles to historical and contemporary issues. Classes earning the highest scores go on to a state level hearing. Oral presentations, before another panel of judges, are based on a new set of hearing and follow-up questions. Each judge scores each group (unit) on a scale of 1–10 (10 being the highest) in six categories using a "Congressional Hearing Group Score Sheet."

193

These six categories are: understanding, constitutional application, reasoning, supporting evidence, responsiveness, and participation.

Judges

At the district level, district coordinators select community members and individuals who have professional background and/or experience with the Constitution (e.g., lawyers, professors, government officials). At the state level, judges are selected who have professional experience with the Constitution and experience serving as judges at the district level. At the national level, judges are nominated by state coordinators.

Winner Notification

District and state winning classes are announced at the end of the scheduled competitive hearing event. Winning classes are announced at an awards banquet in Washington, DC, at the end of a 3-day nation-level hearing.

Awards

At district and state, awards for first, second, and third place are distributed. A Certificate of Achievement is awarded to each school. Awards are given for outstanding performance in each of the six unit topics. Plaques are given to the seven teams placing fourth through tenth. Classes placing first, second, and third receive national recognition from adults and peers at the Gala Awards Banquet. Teachers and students also receive medallions.

Advice

Teachers who participate in the competition thoroughly teach the We the People curriculum. Competing classes are often coached by lawyers, professors, and other professionals.

Competition	**We the Students Scholarship Contest**
Sponsor	Bill of Rights Institute
Web Address	http://billofrightsinstitute.org/programs-events/students-programs-events/scholarship/
Area	Social studies
Competition Origin	1999
Purpose	Educating students about the Bill of Rights and other historical documents.
Description	Students answer three questions about the Bill of Rights with a 500-word essay for each question. The questions can be found on the website.
Eligibility	Students in grades 9–12.
Important Dates	Submission deadline is November 20.
How to Enter	Entries must be submitted online. The submission link is located on the website.
Judging Criteria	Judging based on originality, organization, writing style, and depth of analysis.
Judges	Judges are selected by the Bill of Rights Institute and have knowledge of writing and the Bill of Rights.
Winner Notification	Winners will be announced on the website in February.
Awards	The first-place winner receives a $4,000 scholarship, the second-place winner receives a $2,000 scholarship, the third-place winner receives $1,000, and two Honorable Mention winners each receive a $500 scholarship. In addition, teachers of the first-, second-, and third-place winners receive a cash prize of $100 to put toward classroom resources.
Advice	Check the website to confirm rules and deadlines.

Competition	**The WordMasters Challenge**
Sponsor	WordMasters 5702 N. Pennsylvania Street Indianapolis, IN 46220
Web Address	http://www.wordmasterschallenge.com
Area	Language arts
Competition Origin	1987
Purpose	To encourage growth in vocabulary and verbal reasoning.
Description	Students are challenged to complete analogies based on relationships among the words they have learned through vocabulary development. The contest consists of three 20-minute analogy-solving contests. Guidelines may be obtained on the website or by writing to the sponsor.
Eligibility	Students in grades 3–8 compete in one of two divisions at each grade level. The Blue Division is suitable for students of average to above-average reading and reasoning abilities. The Gold Division is for students who have superior language skills (such as those in gifted and talented programs).
Important Dates	Meets are scheduled during December, February, and April. See guidelines for specific dates.
How to Enter	Schools wishing to participate must register and pay an entrance fee to the sponsor by mid-October.
Judging Criteria	Accuracy of answers.
Judges	Participating teachers and WordMasters officials.
Winner Notification	Winners are notified at the conclusion of each academic year.
Awards	Schools receive 10 certificates of achievement and one Champion Medal to award to top achievers (additional certificates or medals can be purchased on the website).

Competition	**The World Scholar's Cup**
Sponsor	World Scholar's Cup Foundation 1002 Wall Street Los Angeles, CA 90015
Web Address	http://new.scholarscup.org/
Area	Debate, Academic Quiz Bowl, Language Arts
Competition Origin	2006
Purpose	Aims to inspire a global network of diverse students who can use their strengths and skills in creating future communities of scholars and leaders.
Description	Each year, the World Scholar's Cup asks students to learn about, research, and debate serious global issues. In the Team Debate event, teams of three debate with other teams from around the world. Besides the Team Debate, there are three other events: Scholar's Bowl, Collaborative Writing, and the Scholar's Challenge.
Eligibility	Students age 14 and under can participate in the junior division, and students age 15 and older can participate in the senior division. Students can register as a team or individually (students who choose the latter will be paired up with other students).
Important Dates	See the website for dates and locations of competitions available.
How to Enter	Choose a location and register. Complete details of locations and rules are on the website.
Judging Criteria	Debates are judged on effectiveness and relevance to the current theme. The Scholar's Bowl and Scholar's Challenge events are based on the accuracy of answers, and the Collaborative Writing event asks students to write persuasive essays.
Judges	Judges are knowledgeable in a variety of fields.
Winner Notification	Winners are announced at the competition site.
Awards	Trophies and medals are presented to winning teams. Top performing teams from the different worldwide competitions are asked to participate in the Global Round, and top performing teams from the Global Round can participate in the Tournament of Champions.
Advice	Look up current year themes and any updates to regulations on the website

Competition	**The Writers of the Future Contest**
Sponsor	L. Ron Hubbard's Writers of the Future Contest (Author Services, Inc.) P.O. Box 1630 Los Angeles, CA 90078
Web Address	http://www.writersofthefuture.com/
Area	Language arts
Competition Origin	1984
Purpose	To encourage and acknowledge aspiring writers.
Description	This is a contest for writing in the science fiction and fantasy genres. Entries should be under 17,000 words and cannot be poetry or writings intended for children.
Eligibility	The Contest is open only to those who have not professionally published a novel or short novel, or more than one novelette, or more than three short stories, in any medium.
Important Dates	Entries are accepted year round. There are four quarters of competition: the first begins on October 1, the next on January 1, the third on April 1, and the last on July 1.
How to Enter	You may only enter once in each quarter of the year. Material should be typed, double spaced, in black ink on white paper, with numbered pages. Visit the website for full contest rules.
Judging Criteria	Original material that is suitable for publishing. Excessive violence or sexual content as well as plagiarism will disqualify the entry.
Judges	Judges are professional authors. A complete list of current and past judges with short biographies can be found on the website.
Winner Notification	Winners in each quarter will be individually notified of the results by phone, mail, or email.
Awards	Awards of $1,000, $750, and $500 are made quarterly with an annual grand prize of $5,000 awarded to one winner chosen from the quarterly winners. Each winner will also receive a trophy.
Advice	Applicants should check the website for any changes in rules.

Competition	**Young American Creative Patriotic Art Contest**
Sponsor	Ladies Auxiliary to the Veterans of Foreign Wars 406 West 34th St. Kansas City, MO 64111
Web Address	https://www.ladiesauxvfw.org/
Area	Visual arts
Competition Origin	1978
Purpose	To promote patriotism among youth in the United States.
Description	Students submit a piece of art on paper or canvas that is matted. Water color, pencil, pastel, charcoal, tempera, crayon, acrylic, pen-and-ink, or oil may be used. Guidelines can be obtained on the website or by contacting your state chapter.
Eligibility	Students in grades 9–12.
Important Dates	Students should submit their artwork to state chapters by the end of March. The national competition is held in May. See guidelines for specific dates.
How to Enter	Students must enter at state level first. Winners from each state compete in the national competition. Contact your state's chapter for local deadlines.
Judging Criteria	Each entry is judged on the originality of concept, presentation, and patriotism expressed; the content of how it relates to patriotism and clarity of ideas; the design technique; the total impact of work; and uniqueness.
Judges	Those selected to judge the contest on all levels are teachers, professionals, and persons knowledgeable in art.
Winner Notification	Winners are notified prior to the September national meeting.
Awards	State prizes may vary. National scholarships of $10,000, $5,000, and $2,500 are awarded to first-, second-, and third-place winners, respectively. Also, first prize includes a jacket, a plaque, and airfare, plus two nights lodging to attend the Ladies Auxiliary National Convention. The winning art is unveiled at the Convention and featured on the cover of the

Ladies Auxiliary VFW Magazine and on the Ladies Auxiliary website. Second- and third-place winning entries in the National Contest are featured in the Ladies Auxiliary VFW Magazine and on the Auxiliary website.

Competition	**YoungArts Week**
Sponsor	The National YoungArts Foundation (formerly the National Foundation for Advancement in the Arts) 2100 Biscayne Boulevard Miami, FL 33137
Web Address	http://www.youngarts.org
Areas	Performing arts, language arts, and visual arts
Competition Origin	1981
Purpose	To keep culture alive through the development of visual, literary, and performing artists.
Description	Our most talented youth artists meet annually in Miami for YoungArts Week. The top 150 of over 7,000 applicants are given opportunities to attend master classes, workshops, and other enrichment events. The students are judged by a national panel during YoungArts Week to determine the level of award.
Eligibility	Students ages 15–18 years old or in high school, grades 10–12.
Important Dates	Deadlines are in June and October. See guidelines for specific dates.
How to Enter	Applying to the YoungArts program is a 2-step process. First, students must complete the application form online. Upon completion, the student will receive an e-mail with a submission upload link. Then, when ready to upload submission materials (e.g., portfolio, audition video, or other submission materials), students are to follow the specific instructions to complete their submissions.
Judging Criteria	Each submission is evaluated on its own merit in a blind adjudication process by a panel of judges. Panelists adjudicate the annual submissions and identify the national winners in each discipline on each level. Select members of the adjudication panel also work with the finalists during YoungArts Week.
Judges	Judges are comprised of nationally and internationally renowned master artists within each of the nine disciplines in the visual, literary, and performing arts. One panel of experts is present for each art discipline.

Winner Notification

Winners are notified in December.

Awards

Finalists participating in YoungArts Week will be further adjudicated and are eligible to receive awards ranging from $1,000 to $10,000. Honorable Mention winners receive a congratulatory letter and certificate along with a monetary award of $250. Merit winners receive a congratulatory letter and certificate.

Competition	**Young Naturalist Awards**
Sponsor	American Museum of Natural History Central Park West at 79th St. New York, NY 10024-5192
Web Address	http://www.amnh.org/learn-teach/ young-naturalist-awards
Areas	Language arts and science
Competition Origin	1998
Purpose	To encourage students to participate and interact with science.
Description	Students write a research-based narrative essay on a certain topic. They explore and collect data on this topic. Guidelines may be obtained on the website or by writing to the sponsor.
Eligibility	Students in grades 7–12.
Important Dates	Students may start submitting entries in December through to the end of March. See guidelines for specific dates.
Judging Criteria	Entries are judged according to the student's investigation, procedure, analysis, interpretation, research materials, clarity of the report, and style of writing.
Judges	Museum scientists.
Winner Notification	Winners are notified in the spring.
Awards	Twelve cash awards, two for each grade level, will be awarded to the authors of the winning essays. Cash awards range from $500 to $2,500. The winning entries are published on the Museum's website. Up to 36 finalists receive a cash award of $50 and a certificate of recognition. Up to 200 semifinalists receive a noncash award and a certificate of recognition. The teachers of the top 12 winners receive classroom resources and a free Seminars on Science course.

Competition	**Young Playwrights Inc. National Playwriting Competition**
Sponsor	Young Playwrights Inc. P.O. Box 5134 New York, NY 10185
Web Address	http://www.youngplaywrights.org/national-competition/
Areas	Language arts and performing arts
Competition Origin	1981
Purpose	To introduce young people to the theater and to encourage self-expression through the art of playwriting.
Description	Students submit an original play that will be read and evaluated by a theater professional. Guidelines may be obtained on the website or by writing to the sponsor.
Eligibility	Students ages 18 and younger (as of deadline).
Important Dates	The deadline for entry is early January. See guidelines for specific dates.
How to Enter	Obtain the guidelines and submit an original playscript according to the guidelines. Screenplays, musicals, and adaptations are not eligible. More than one play may be submitted.
Judging Criteria	Selections are based on the quality of writing in playwriting competition. Each playwright receives a written evaluation of the work submitted.
Judges	Judges are made up of theater professionals.
Winner Notification	Notification of preliminary selections is made in the spring. Final selections take place in early summer.
Awards	Production of the play Off Broadway in the Young Playwrights Festival. Authors participate in casting and rehearsal of their plays. Playwrights also receive transportation, housing, royalties, and complimentary 1-year membership in the Dramatists Guild.

Competition	**Youth for Understanding International Exchange**
Sponsor	Youth for Understanding USA 6400 Goldsboro Road, Ste. 100 Bethesda, MD 20817
Web Address	http://www.yfu-usa.org
Area	Academic recognition and foreign language
Competition Origin	1952
Purpose	To provide scholarships for students to participate in international exchanges.
Description	Youth for Understanding International Exchange administers full or partial scholarship programs for American students to study overseas. Guidelines may be obtained on the website or by writing to the sponsor.
Eligibility	Students ages 15–18.
Important Dates	Scholarship applications are due between December and February. See guidelines for specific dates.
How to Enter	Students must complete an application form and be nominated by a principal, teacher, or guidance counselor.
Judging Criteria	For most year and semester programs, a B average or better (3.0 on a 4.0 scale) is required. For summer programs, a C average or better (2.0 on a 4.0 scale) is required; however, a 3.0 GPA or higher may be required in some cases.
Judges	Corporate sponsors for each scholarship.
Winner Notification	Winners are notified prior to the start of program.
Awards	Scholarships include • professional orientation programs and materials; • all group international air travel costs and assistance from YFU travel staff at international gateway airports; • domestic air travel costs from a YFU-designated airport; • local and regional trips and educational activities while you're overseas (where noted); • placement with a carefully screened YFU host family;

- support through counseling, tutoring, and other means;
- training for volunteers who provide professional, individual support for you and your host family;
- 24-hour worldwide professional emergency assistance;
- enrollment in school if your scholarship is for a year or semester program;
- assistance in acquiring your visa or residence permit if required;
- the 1-800-TEENAGE line staffed with friendly and knowledgeable Admissions Counselors to answer all of your questions.

Advice

Many scholarships are designated for a specific country. Others allow you to list several country choices. You should think carefully about which countries interest you most.

PART II
COMPETITIONS JOURNAL

Why I Want to Enter a Competition

Think of the many great reasons you want to enter competitions. List them and keep them in mind throughout your preparation and participation in competitions.

_____

_____

_____

_____

_____

_____

_____

_____

_____

_____

_____

_____

_____

_____

_____

_____

_____

_____

_____

Top 10 Competitions I'd Like to Enter

What competitions interest you? In which competitions can you see yourself as a terrific participant? Choose your top 10 competitions and list them in rank order from your most favorite to your least favorite. As you begin competing you can change your list.

_____

_____

_____

_____

_____

_____

_____

_____

_____

_____

_____

_____

_____

_____

_____

_____

_____

_____

Letter or E-mail to Obtain Competition Information

From time to time you may hear of additional competitions or need more information on a specific one. A short e-mail requesting the details will usually get a quick reply. If you send a physical letter, be sure to include a self-addressed, stamped envelope. Some competitions may not reply to your letter if this is not included. This sample correspondence will serve as a guide for you.

Date

Your Name
Street Address
City, State   Zip Code

Competition Name
Street Address
City, State   Zip Code

Dear (insert name of contact if known; otherwise use Sir or Madam),

The (insert name of competition) competition is of interest to me and I would like to request more information. Please send me any materials you might have on the purpose, requirements, and awards. Thank you for responding to this request.

Sincerely,

Your name

My Competition Goals

What are your competition goals? In which competitions would you like to be involved? What skills would you like to sharpen? With whom would you like to meet and share your ideas? Competitions can lead to the accomplishment of many personal goals. Find a nice quiet place to sit and think about your goals and how you plan to achieve them through competitions. Write down your thoughts. As you meet your goals, decide on new ones.

Goal: _____

Steps to achieving my goal:

_____

_____

_____

_____

_____

Goal: _____

Steps to achieving my goal:

_____

_____

_____

_____

_____

The Spirit of Competition!

Think about the spirit of competition . . . specifically yours! How do you feel or think you will feel before, during, and after a competition? Write down the ways you feel and the causes of those feelings.

Before a competition, I may feel or have felt . . .

_____

_____

_____

During a competition, I may feel or have felt . . .

_____

_____

_____

After a competition, I may feel or have felt . . .

_____

_____

_____

Things I can do to make myself feel better . . .

_____

_____

_____

How I Selected a Competition

Reflect upon the process you went through in order to select a competition in which you want to participate or have done so. List the many reasons for your selection. You may want to add to this list with each new competition you enter.

My talents and abilities:

_____

_____

My interests:

_____

_____

My resources:

_____

_____

The guidelines:

_____

_____

Awards:

_____

_____

Other:

_____

Time Management Tips

As you begin planning for and participating in competitions, you'll quickly find the importance and value of managing your time well. You can do it by following these tips. As you learn to manage your time, write down what works for you—your very own time management tips.

Set priorities. Decide what is the most important task and do it first. It may help to write down your goals in order of importance.

Be flexible. Remember, sometimes things change. Take advantage of opportunities to try something different.

Plan time to get organized. Just getting organized takes a few minutes. Grab your calendar, list of goals, and competition information; find a comfortable place to sit; and start organizing and planning.

Use little bits of time. There are times you can use to complete small jobs, like waiting on the bus, TV commercial breaks during your favorite show, or in between classes. Find something small and get it done.

Set deadlines. Decide when you'd like to have your goals met. Be sure to check off each one as you complete it. If you finish before a deadline, good for you!

Make and use lists. Write down your plans for getting ready for the competition. As you finish each step, celebrate by marking it off.

Use calendars or appointment books. These are great tools for staying on top of things. A sample calendar is provided in this book. Use it or one of your own.

My time management tips:

_____

_____

_____

_____

My Competition Calendar

Keeping important dates straight is one of the keys to success in competition. Depending upon your individual style and preference, a calendar of some sort will help you do just that. There are many different types of calendars: pocket, wall, weekly, and monthly, to name a few. Computers, tablets, and smartphones also come with calendar programs. Whether physical or digital, select the one that's best for you.

Here is a sample:

Day of Week	Things to Do Today
Sunday	
Monday	
Tuesday	
Wednesday	
Thursday	
Friday	
Saturday	

Things I Need for the Competition

As you prepare for a competition, think about the items you will need for success. List the items you will need, marking those you have and those you will have to acquire. Determine where you will get those items you don't yet have.

Items required:	I have these:	I'll have to get these from:

Phone Calls

The telephone can be a great tool for asking questions and finding answers, networking with others, and sharing good news. It's important to use good phone manners. Plan your conversation and be certain to write down any important information you receive. This phone form may help you.

"Hello, my name is (your name). May I please speak to (name of person) or someone who can give me information about the (name of competition)?"

"I am calling (state the reason you are calling) . . . " You should prepare what you are going to say ahead of time. Use the space below to write down your thoughts.

_____

_____

_____

_____

What information did you receive? Write down what you are told by your contact.

_____

_____

_____

_____

"Thank you very much. I appreciate your help." After you have received the needed information, be sure to conclude the call by letting the person know that you appreciate his or her time and help.

Be sure to write the date and time of the call, as well as the name and phone number of the person with whom you spoke.

Date and time: _____

Contact person's name:_____

Contact person's phone number: _____

Sponsor, Sponsor . . . Who's Got a Sponsor?

Competitions sometimes require a school or community sponsor. Other times, sponsors can be located to give support in terms of advice, money, and/or time and goods/services. But how do you get a sponsor? It's easy. Just follow these steps!

Gather all the facts and details about the competition in which you are interested. Read about it. Be sure you clearly understand the competition.

Write down exactly why you need a sponsor and what you need the sponsor to do. Think about what you will say when you speak to the potential sponsor. You might even want to practice the conversation with someone else.

Brainstorm individuals or businesses in your school and community who may be willing and able to help you. You may want to ask your parents, teachers, or friends to assist you as you put together this list.

You may want to look online or in the yellow pages of your telephone directory or contact the local Chamber of Commerce for possible sponsors.

Contact the sponsor by e-mail, phone, or letter. Ask if you can set up an appointment or special time to meet so that you can discuss your competition plans and ideas.

Go visit your sponsor. Be sure you are on time and look nice. Manners are important, too, so use only the best. Notes and information about the competition may be helpful, so take them. You might want to have an extra copy to leave with the possible sponsor. Smile!

Be sure to thank your sponsor after the contest is over. A little thanks goes a long way. Remember to let them know how much you enjoyed being a part of the contest in which you entered. Write a thank you note with details of the competition you were able to enter with their help.

Great Lessons I've Learned

Competitions can teach us a lot of things about our interests, our strengths, our abilities, and ourselves. We can learn more about our work habits, attitudes, and goals for the future as we meet others, plan projects, and have fun. Think about the great lessons you will learn or have learned through competition.

Through competition I will learn . . .	Through competition I have learned more about . . .
My interests:	My interests:
My strengths:	My strengths:
My abilities:	My abilities:
My attitudes:	My attitudes:
My work habits:	My work habits:
My goals:	My goals:

My List of Recognitions

There are many different kinds of recognition given for participation in competitions. You may receive a medal, trophy, certificate,
money, or even a trip. What types of recognition would you like to
receive? Better yet, how have you already been recognized?

List of Recognitions I Have Already Received	List of Recognitions I Would Like to Receive

My Slogan for Competitions

What are your feelings and attitudes about competitions? Sum it all up in a slogan. Write a catchy, creative slogan for competitions. Share your ideas with others through a poster, T-shirt design, a bumper sticker, or a play—the possibilities are endless.

_____

_____

_____

_____

_____

_____

_____

_____

_____

_____

_____

_____

_____

_____

_____

_____

_____

Competitions Are Fun

Planning and participating in competitions will involve work, but you'll also have tons of fun. You will use your mind in new ways, learn to develop a variety of products, meet new friends, develop and enhance your personal and social skills, and perhaps travel to new and different places. Keeping these memories of all the fun activities will be great. Perhaps you'll want to share these exciting experiences with your friends through discussions, letters, e-mail, a blog, editorials in your school or local newspaper, a TV or radio interview, or a dozen other ways.

Ways I've had fun through competitions:

_____

_____

_____

_____

_____

_____

_____

_____

_____

_____

_____

_____

_____

_____

Being Recognized

Being in competitions may bring recognition to you, your school, and your community. A great way to share your accomplishments is through a press release to be sent to newspapers, television, and/or radio. Look in your local telephone book for the addresses. You may use the format below to notify others of your accomplishments.

PRESS RELEASE

(Your name) participated in the (competition name) on (date) in (city, state). (He/She) is a (your grade) grade student at (your school) in (city, state). The (competition name) is designed to (purpose of competition). (Add more detailed information as you see fit.)

Thank You Letter

Thank you letters are a great way to show your appreciation to the many people who have been encouraging and supportive of you when entering a competition. You may want to write to your teacher, sponsor, parents, friends, and others. Don't forget to say kind words to the people who were responsible for running the competition. They have worked hard to make it a great event.

Here is a sample thank you note. You'll want to use your own special way of expressing your appreciation.

Date

Your Name
Street Address
City, State   Zip Code

Competition or Contact's Name
Street Address
City, State   Zip Code

Dear (insert name of contact if known; otherwise use Sir or Madam),

Thank you for the opportunity to participate in (name of competition). I learned (mention what you have learned from participating in this competition). You were very helpful, and I appreciate (cite something specific that you appreciate). (Add more information as needed.)

Sincerely,

Your name

What Else Is Out There?

There are many opportunities available for you to share your talents and abilities through competitions. We've given you quite a few national ones from which to choose, but there may be others you'd like to try. As you discover local, regional, state, and national contests of interest, record the information. Share these other contests with your friends. Use a program like Microsoft Excel to create a database of competitions, and update it regularly. Your spreadsheet may look something like this:

Competition	Contact Person	Address	Area of Competition	Date

Start a Competition Club

Wouldn't it be fun to share your successes and good ideas with your friends? Why not start a competition club? You and your fellow members can share information about upcoming contests, discuss the ups and downs of competing, and best of all, form a network of friends. Before starting your club, think about the following questions.

What will be the purpose of your club?

_____

_____

_____

Who will be able to join your club?

_____

_____

_____

How will new members join?

_____

_____

_____

When and where will your club meet?

_____

_____

_____

Who will help you get your club started?

_____

_____

_____

How will you let others know about your club?

_____

_____

_____

How will you obtain permission to start a club, if indeed permission is needed?

_____

_____

_____

How will you keep the club going?

_____

_____

_____

Will you charge a membership fee?

_____

_____

_____

Let's Hear From You!

You are important to us and we would like to hear from you! Please share your ideas and comments about this book and your participation in competitions. We encourage you to write to us.

I am a:
- ❑ student
- ❑ teacher
- ❑ guidance counselor
- ❑ school administrator
- ❑ competition director
- ❑ other

1. What is your favorite competition and why?

_____

_____

2. What have you learned by participating in competition(s)?

_____

_____

3. If you have participated in national competitions other than the ones listed in this book, please share the information.

_____

_____

Name of Competition: _____

Address: _____

City, State, Zip: _____

4. What suggestions do you have for additional information for this book?

_____

_____

5. Other comments

_____

_____

Mail this form to:
Dr. Frances A. Karnes
University of Southern Mississippi
118 College Drive
Box 8207
Hattiesburg, MS 39406-8207

PART III
RESOURCES

Photography and Video

- *Basic 35MM Photo Guide: For Beginning Photographers* by Craig Alesse
- *The Klutz Book of Animation: How to Make Your Own Stop Motion Movies* by Nicholas Berger and John Cassiday
- *The Kids' Guide to Digital Photography: How to Shoot, Save, Play With & Print Your Digital Photos* by Jenni Bidner
- *National Geographic Photography Field Guide: Secrets to Making Great Pictures (Second Edition)* by Peter Burian and Robert Caputo
- *Photography for Kids! A Fun Guide to Digital Photography* by Michael Ebert and Sandra Abend
- *I Wanna Take Me a Picture: Teaching Photography and Writing to Children* by Wendy Ewald and Alexandra Lightfoot
- *Picture This: Fun Photography and Crafts* by Debra Friedman
- *Digital Photo Madness! 50 Weird and Wacky Things to Do With Your Digital Camera* by Thom Gaines
- *The New Manual of Photography* by John Hedgecoe
- *Tricky Pix: Do-It-Yourself Tricky Photography* by Paula Weed and Carla Jimison
- *4-H Guide to Digital Photography* by Daniel Johnson
- *National Geographic Photography Guide for Kids* by Neil Johnson
- *Cameras: All About Series* by Chris Oxlade

Speeches

- *Oral Presentations Made Easy: Super Strategies and Warm-ups That Help Kids Write and Give Effective Speeches and Presentations— and Communicate With Confidence* by Bob Barlow
- *A Student's Guide to Presentations: Making Your Presentation Count* by Barbara Chivers and Michael Shoolbred
- *How to Deliver a TED Talk: Secrets of the World's Most Inspiring Presentations* by Jeremey Donovan

- *Speakers' Club: Public Speaking for Young People* by Barbara Juskow
- *Speaking Up Without Freaking Out: 35 Techniques for Confident, Calm, and Competent Presenting* by Matt Abrahams
- *Speak Out! Debate and Public Speaking in the Middle Grades* by John Meany and Kate Shuster
- *Public Speaking: 7 Steps to Writing and Delivering a Great Speech (A Student Guide)* by Katherine Pebley O'Neal

Visual Arts

- *Cartooning for Kids* by Mike Artell
- *Charcoal Pocket Studio* by Patrick Bullock and Patsy North
- *My Animal Art Class* by Nellie Shepherd
- *My Art Class: Kitchen Crafts* by Nellie Shepherd
- *Creative Crafts for Kids* by Gill Dickerson and Cheryl Owen
- *I Can Draw It Myself by Me, Myself* by Dr. Seuss
- *Draw 3-D* by Doug DuBosque
- *How to Draw and Paint People* by Angela Cair
- *You Can Draw Anything* by Kim Gamble
- *The Usborne Book of Papier Mache* by Ray Gibson
- *Kids Draw Animals* by Christopher Hart
- *How to Make Super Pop-Ups* by Joan Irvine and Linda Hendry
- *Dare to Draw in 3-D: Cartoon Critters* by Mark Kistler
- *Drawing Cartoons (Usborne Art Ideas)* by Anna Milbourne
- *The Usborne Complete Book of Art Ideas* by Fiona Watt and Antonia Miller
- *Henri Matisse: Drawing With Scissors* by Jane O'Connor and Jessie Hartland
- *The Usborne Book of Graphic Design* by Peach Potter
- *Artistic Drawing (Creative Kids)* by Kat Rakel-Ferguson
- *Anatomy for the Artist* by Sarah Simblet
- *The Usborne Complete Book of Drawing* by Nigel Reece, Alastair Smith, and Judy Tatchell

- *Art for Kids: Drawing: The Only Drawing Book You'll Ever Need to Be the Artist You've Always Wanted to Be* by Kathryn Temple
- *The Usborne Book of Drawing, Doodling, and Coloring* by Fiona Watt

Writing

- *The Young Author's Do-It-Yourself Book* by Donna Guthrie, Nancy Bentley, and Katy Keck Arnsteen
- *What's Your Story? A Young Person's Guide to Writing Fiction* by Marion Dane Bauer
- *Rip the Page! Adventures in Creative Writing* by Karen Benke
- *A Teen's Guide to Getting Published: Publishing for Profit, Recognition, and Academic Success* by Jessica Dunn and Danielle Dunn
- *How Writers Work: Finding a Process That Works for You* by Ralph Fletcher
- *Poetry Matters: Writing a Poem From the Inside Out* by Ralph Fletcher
- *Writing Skills Made Fun: Parts of Speech* by Karen Kellaher
- *Writing Your Own Plays: Creating, Adapting, Improvising* by Carol Korty
- *Spilling Ink: A Young Writer's Handbook* by Ellen Potter and Anne Mazer
- *Seize the Story* by Victoria Hanley

about the authors

Frances A. Karnes, Ph.D., is a distinguished professor of curriculum, instruction, and special education at The University of Southern Mississippi and director of the Frances A. Karnes Center for Gifted Studies. She is widely known for her research, writing, innovative program developments, and service activities in gifted education and leadership training. She is author or coauthor of more than 200 articles and coauthor or coeditor of 71 books on gifted education and related areas. Dr. Karnes is the former president of The Association for the Gifted and is the founder and first president of the Mississippi Association for Gifted Children, and she has served on the board of the National Association for Gifted Children. Honors include a Faculty Research Award, granted by The University of Southern Mississippi Alumni Association; an honorary doctor of education degree from her alma mater Quincy University; and an award presented by the Mississippi Legislature for outstanding contributions to academic excellence in higher education. She has received the Power of One Award bestowed by the governor of Mississippi and was named one of 50 female business leaders by the *Mississippi Business Journal.* In 2007, she received the Lifetime Achievement Award from The University of Southern Mississippi.

Tracy L. Riley, Ph.D., is an associate professor who specializes in gifted and talented education. She teaches undergraduate and postgraduate courses in the field in addition to supervising postgraduate research. Tracy is the coeditor of *APEX: The New Zealand Journal of Gifted Education* and is on the editorial board of *Gifted Child*

Today. An active advocate for gifted and talented students, Tracy has served on numerous Ministry of Education advisory groups and has coauthored the Ministry handbook, *Gifted and Talented Students: Meeting Their Needs in New Zealand Schools.* She publishes and presents widely at both national and international levels. In 2007, Tracy was awarded the Vice-Chancellor's Award for Sustained Excellence in Teaching and was the recipient of a national Tertiary Teaching Excellence Award. Tracy is a member of the executive committee of the Ako Aoteoroa Academy of Tertiary Teaching Excellence and is chairperson of the board for giftEDnz, The Professional Association for Gifted Education.